The Gift of Dyslexia

Why Some of the Brightest People Can't Read and How They Can Learn

Ronald D. Davis
with Eldon M. Braun

SOUVENIR PRESS

In honour and memory of
Harold Joseph Anderson
one man who cared

First published in the USA by
Ability Workshop Press, Burlingame, California

First British edition published 1995 by
Souvenir Press Ltd,
43 Great Russell Street, London WC1B 3PA
Reprinted 1996 (twice)
Second edition, revised and enlarged, 1997
Reprinted 1998

ISBN 0 285 63412 7

Photoset by Rowland Phototypesetting Ltd
Bury St Edmunds, Suffolk
Printed in Great Britain by
Creative Print and Design Wales, Ebbw Vale

Illustrations by Mia Sutter
Photographs by P. Courtney Davis
Computer graphics by Mark Gittus

This book is intentionally typeset in larger than
normal type and with the fewest possible word breaks
in order to make it dyslexic-friendly.

Contents

Foreword   *by Dr Joan Smith*   v

Acknowledgements   xi

Preface   xiii

PART ONE
What Dyslexia Really Is

Chapter 1   The Underlying Talent   3

Chapter 2   The Learning Disability   8

Chapter 3   Effects of Disorientation   15

Chapter 4   Dyslexia in Action   21

Chapter 5   Compulsive Solutions   29

Chapter 6   Problems with Reading   34

Chapter 7   Spelling Problems   40

Chapter 8   Maths Problems   43

Chapter 9   Handwriting Problems   47

Chapter 10   The Newest Disability: ADD   54

Chapter 11   Clumsiness   61

Chapter 12   A Real Solution   64

PART TWO
Little P.D.—A Developmental
Theory of Dyslexia

Chapter 13   How Dyslexia Happens   73

Chapter 14   The Two-Year-Old and the Kitten   78

Chapter 15   Ages Three to Five   81

Chapter 16   The First Day of School   84
Chapter 17   The Age of Disability   90

PART THREE
The Gift

Chapter 18   Understanding the Talent   99
Chapter 19   Curiosity   106
Chapter 20   Creativity   109
Chapter 21   The Gift of Mastery   113

PART FOUR
Doing Something About It

Chapter 22   How Can You Tell?   119
Chapter 23   Symptoms of Disorientation   124
Chapter 24   The Mind's Eye   129
Chapter 25   Implementing the Davis Procedures   135
Chapter 26   Perceptual Ability Assessment   141
Chapter 27   Turning It Round   151
Chapter 28   Release and Review   180
Chapter 29   Fine Tuning   187
Chapter 30   Coordination   195
Chapter 31   Basic Symbol Mastery   198
Chapter 32   Three Steps to Easier Reading   215
Chapter 33   Symbol Mastery for Words   224
Chapter 34   Continuing the Process   237

Glossary   242
Recommended References   249
Davis Dyslexia Association International (DDAI)   253
Index   256

Foreword

During my 25 years of experience in working with students who have learning disabilities, I have learned that it is always the student who teaches me what I need to know. Therefore, it is no surprise to me that a dyslexic individual has come forward to teach us what we need to know about dyslexia.

As a student, Ron Davis suffered the injustices, unfair treatment and humiliation familiar to most individuals with the unique learning style called dyslexia. The combination of talents and inefficiencies described in Ron's book will be recognised immediately by others who possess this unique combination of skills and difficulties.

As a teacher, Ron Davis provides us with an experiential, first-person understanding of what the dyslexic student encounters. He describes how learning differs for the dyslexic individual in words we can understand. He makes the experience real and, in so doing, gives us the insights necessary to teach effectively.

Four different learning locks are opened by the keys of Ron's accomplishments:

1   The key to understanding that the dyslexic learning style is actually a talent.

2   The key to comprehending the dimensional awareness of the dyslexic individual.

3   The key to conceptualising disorientation.

4   The key to techniques which control disorientation, thereby controlling the dyslexic symptoms.

A wide variety of symptoms is manifested by the dyslexic syndrome. For that reason, experts in different fields provide a variety of definitions. The most frequently recognised characteristics include severe reading, spelling and writing delays, and reversals of symbols. Other symptoms of the dyslexic syndrome include time and space confusion, disorganisation, and difficulty with comprehension.

Some dyslexics find that they are totally unable to learn to read. As adults, they still struggle with putting sounds and letters together to decode words. They cannot recall symbols or combinations of symbols. Words they know do not look familiar on the page. Their level of ability to recognise words is usually that of a nine-year-old, even though they may have had years of reading intervention.

Other individuals can read words fairly well. When reading aloud, they sound coherent. But these students find that they cannot understand what they read. They must go over a sentence several times in order to glean some meaning from it. They tend to experience severe difficulty in writing, and find the symbols of language very frustrating.

Both types of dyslexics experience the same humiliation and frustration. They are technically illiterate and limited in their freedom to make the printed word work for them.

These individuals have always provided a strong motivation for teachers and researchers. Their disabilities in reading and using their intelligence in a traditional manner have inspired our organisation to continue seeking answers and solutions to their discomfort. In our efforts to assist our clients at the Melvin-Smith Learning Center, we investigate any and all techniques that appear.

In 1983, a dyslexic student from our school's programme was taken by his parents to Ron Davis' Reading Research Council. This was our first introduction to a truly unique programme. When the student returned to school, he was definitely 'on a high' from his success. He claimed that he could concentrate and stay on task for the first time.

I immediately questioned him about what it was that had made such a difference. 'I can't tell you, Dr Smith,' he informed me. 'It might make you sick. Only dyslexic people can do this. It makes other people sick.' I now understand that he was referring to the Orientation Counselling he had received, and the side effect of queasiness that *dis*orientation can sometimes have on people who are not dyslexic. But at the time, I was both confused and sceptical. I decided to wait and observe him to determine whether any lasting changes appeared in his learning patterns.

What I observed was a student whose ability to focus on studies was obviously improved. By the end of his last year, he was accepted into a prestigious secondary school, and apparently he was successful. He demonstrated consistently improved levels of confidence, and gradually changed in his reading and writing skills as he participated in the Word and Symbol Mastery programme.

Two years later, I encountered another student who was about to attend the Reading Research Council programme. This time, things were different. I was invited to come along and learn the techniques which would be used to tutor her after her training programme. My curiosity had already been aroused, so I was eager to experience the programme first hand.

After what I saw, I decided to become trained in the Davis Orientation Counselling processes and Symbol Mastery techniques. Subsequently, more teachers on our staff have taken the training, and we use these techniques regularly at the Melvin-Smith Learning Center.

The Davis concept of 'orientation' is most easily

recognised by teachers and psychologists as 'attention'. Orientation Counselling provides the client with a stabilisation and a point of reference for the focus of attention. This is essentially to prevent disorientation and confusion in working with symbols for reading, writing, spelling, speaking and even computation. A strong visual stabilisation takes place which benefits attention focus and creates the feeling of 'control' reported by most individuals. Gaining control of and being in charge of one's learning system is essential to learning, especially when something as complex as a reading system is being learned.

The presentation of the dyslexic learning style as a talent is correct. For years, we have observed that individuals who experience dyslexic symptoms are highly intelligent. The talents that create the vulnerability for confusing symbolic information are assets in other ways. For example, individuals who 'see' the dimensional attributes in our world understand intuitively how things work. They find that they have an innate ability for fixing things, understanding engines, electronics, plumbing, construction, visual arts and other related fields. Tasks which require the ability to visualise something in a creative or different way are often simple for the individual with these talents. This is most likely why so many inventors, scientists, athletes and creative individuals find that they also have dyslexic symptoms.

After Orientation Counselling, the Symbol Mastery techniques developed by Ron Davis are utilised to improve the student's reading and writing skills, primarily by resolving confusions about letters, words, numbers, punctuation marks and mathematical symbols. These procedures have an excellent foundation in learning theory. They use each of the senses for learning and provide for concept integration. Students see, touch, discuss and conceptualise the information they are learning. The application of a strong multisensory approach provides stimulation of important parts of the brain and facilitates long term retention.

The keys Ron has given us for the four learning locks mentioned previously have benefited our clients and advanced our research into the understanding of the dyslexic syndrome. Because of our increased understanding, we have developed more effective ways of explaining the dyslexic experience to our clients' families, friends and employers, and to the individuals themselves. The confirmation provided by our clients is reassuring and inspires confidence that the diagnosis is correct. A shared understanding of what is being experienced by the individual becomes possible.

When they receive the information following their assessment, clients fequently say, 'That's it. That's what I experience.' At this point, their isolation and confusion are released. They are ready to experience the changes which can accompany a therapeutic programme.

In combining the roles of student and teacher in this book Ron enriches our understanding of millions of individuals who experience the unique learning style known as dyslexia. Ron's work has provided us with a means for understanding the dyslexic learner. He has developed a set of effective techniques for meeting unique learning needs which in turn have given us new hope of success.

Joan M. Smith, Ed.D.
Licensed Educational Psychologist
Licensed Speech Pathologist

Dr Joan Smith is Educational Director of the Melvin-Smith Learning Centers, with corporate offices in Sacramento, California. She is the author and co-author of numerous books and articles on special education. Her latest publication is You Don't Have to Be Dyslexic.

Acknowledgements

Even though Eldon Braun and I have our names on this book, we are not its only creators. My wife Alice has worked just as hard as either of us to put this book in your hands. In addition to being our editor, she has been the mediator of conflicts, the soother of ruffled feathers and the doctor of bruised egos.

Two others deserve special thanks: Dr Fatima Ali, who has been the CEO of the Reading Research Council and my mentor since 1981; and Larry J. Rochester, without whose help we would have never got started.

Others who have given inspiration, commitment and support include:

Rakaia Ansari	*The Rev. Beth Gray*
Dr Richard Blasband	*Chris Jackson*
Alease Helmick Davis	*Betty Ann and Dehlia Judah*
Courtney Davis	*Keith and June Monaghan*
Sarah Derr	*Vickie Morgan*
Jim Evers	*Jacqueline Pratt*
Bill and Charlotte Foster	*Dana Rahlmann*
Dr Louis Gann	*Marilyn Rosenthal*
Jeff Gershow	*Dr Barry Schwartz*
Dr Albrecht Giese	*Dr Joan Smith*
Larry and Susan Gilbert	*Jill Stowell*
Dr Brian Halevie-Goldman	*Dorothy Towner*

Finally, my thanks to the thousands of dyslexics who have walked through the doors of the Reading Research Council and to those who continue to show up each week. It is they who are answering my prayer and helping me finally get out of my corner.

Preface

The clock on the classroom wall ticks slower and slower. Tick . . . tick . . . . . . tick . . . .

'Please hurry! Please hurry! Please—please—please hurry!' The young boy's whispered words are barely audible. Every muscle in his body is tense. His fingers twitch and tremble. His knees, pressed tightly together, quiver and touch the walls of the corner. He rocks slowly back and forth, but is careful not to dislodge the folded white handkerchief, his label of unworthiness, draped like a flag across the top of his head.

'Please—please!' he whispers again. Then he sucks in his breath and winces. But it doesn't help, nothing can. Within minutes it starts, a trickle at first, then all of it. He silently hopes there isn't so much that it makes a puddle on the floor.

He hunches over, pressing his face tight into the corner. His wrists cross into an X in his lap, hoping to hide the wet spot. Now he is glad he won't be leaving the school when the other kids do. Maybe they'll all be gone when he leaves and nobody will see; nobody will tease him. He has hoped this hope at least a hundred times before, but maybe this time he won't hear those awful words:

'Half-wit!'

'Moron!'

'Look at the nutter.'

'Nutty's wet himself again.'

He is startled by the bell that signals school is over for the day. In the corner, amidst the clatter and clamour of the children leaving, the boy sits motionless, hoping nobody will look in his direction. If he could be invisible he would be. Not until the room is quiet does he dare move, does he dare make a sound.

As the noise fades, the ticking of the clock accelerates. Tick . . . tick, tick!

Under his breath, the boy whispers something that only he should hear.

'What did you say?' The loud voice booms right behind him.

If he hadn't already done it, he would be wetting himself now. He presses into the corner as tightly as he can and tries to be as small as he can be.

One of the hands that put him in the corner grabs his shoulder and pulls him round. 'What did you say?' the voice demands.

'I asked God not to make me sit in the corner any more.'

That child's prayer is the sole reason for this book.

PART ONE

What Dyslexia Really Is

CHAPTER 1

The Underlying Talent

Usually when people hear the word *dyslexia* they think only of the reading, writing, spelling and maths problems a child is having in school. Some associate it only with word and letter reversals, some only with slow learners. Almost everyone considers it some form of learning disability, but the learning disability is only one face of dyslexia.

Once as a guest on a television show I was asked about the 'positive' side of dyslexia. As part of my answer, I listed a dozen or so famous dyslexics. The hostess of the show then commented, 'Isn't it amazing that all those people could be geniuses in spite of having dyslexia.'

She missed the point. Their genius didn't occur *in spite* of their dyslexia, but *because* of it!

Having dyslexia won't make every dyslexic a genius, but it is good for the self-esteem of all dyslexics to know that their minds work in exactly the same way as the minds of great geniuses. It is

Some Talented Dyslexics

Inventors/Engineers/ Scientists	*Albert Einstein* *Thomas Edison* *Alexander Graham Bell*
Artists/Writers	*Leonardo da Vinci* *Walt Disney* *Hans Christian Andersen* *W. B. Yeats*
Military/Political Strategists	*General George Patton* *Winston Churchill* *Michael Heseltine*
Performers	*Cher* *Whoopi Goldberg* *Susan Hampshire*
Athletes	*Jackie Stewart* *Duncan Goodhew*

also important for them to know that having a problem with reading, writing, spelling or maths doesn't mean they are stupid. The same mental function that produces a genius can also produce those problems.

The mental function that causes dyslexia is a gift in the truest sense of the world: *a natural ability, a talent*. It is something special that enhances the individual.

Dyslexics don't all develop the same gifts, but

they do have certain mental functions in common. Here are the basic abilities all dyslexics share:

1 They can utilise the brain's ability to alter and create perceptions (the primary ability).

2 They are highly aware of the environment.

3 They are more curious than average.

4 They think mainly in pictures instead of words.

5 They are highly intuitive and perceptive.

6 They think and perceive multidimensionally (using all the senses).

7 They can experience thought as reality.

8 They have vivid imaginations.

These eight basic abilities, if not suppressed, invalidated or destroyed by parents or the educational process, will result in two characteristics: higher than normal intelligence, and extraordinary creative abilities. From these the true gift of dyslexia can emerge—the gift of mastery.

The gift of mastery develops in many ways and in many areas. For Albert Einstein it was physics; for Walt Disney it was art; for Susan Hampshire it was acting ability.

A PARADIGM SHIFT

To change our perspective of dyslexia from disability to gift we must start with a clear, accurate under-standing of what dyslexia really is, and what causes it. Doing this will bring out the positive as well as the negative aspects of the situation and allow us to see how dyslexia develops. Then the idea of correcting it won't seem far-fetched. Going a step beyond correcting the problem, we can also recognise and explore this condition as the gift it truly is.

Before a dyslexic person can fully realise and appreciate the positive side of dyslexia, the negative side should be addressed. That doesn't mean the positive side will not surface until the problems are solved. The gift is always there, even if it isn't recognised for what it is. In fact, many adult dyslexics use the positive side of dyslexia in their careers without realising it. They just think they have a *knack* of doing something, without realising that their special talent comes from the same mental functions that prevent them from being able to read, write or spell very well.

The most common disabilities of dyslexia occur in reading, writing, spelling or maths; but there are many others. Each case of dyslexia is different, because dyslexia is a *self-created condition*. No two dyslexics have created it in exactly the same way.

In order to understand the *gift of dyslexia*, we

need to view the learning disability known as dyslexia from a different angle.

Dyslexia is the result of a perceptual talent. In some situations, the talent becomes a liability. The individual doesn't realise this is happening because use of the talent has become integrated into the thought process. It began very early in life and by now seems as natural as breathing.

CHAPTER 2

The Learning Disability

Dyslexia was the first general term used to describe various learning problems. Eventually, these problems were subdivided and categorised to describe different learning disabilities. Because of this, we might call dyslexia the Mother of Learning Disabilities. By now, over seventy names are used to describe its various aspects.

Originally, researchers thought dyslexic people had some form of brain or nerve damage, or a congenital malfunction that interfered with the mental processes necessary for reading.

Then, in the late 1920s, Dr Samuel Torrey Orton redefined dyslexia as 'cross lateralisation of the brain'. This meant that the left side of the brain was doing what the right side was normally supposed to do, and the right side was doing the job of the left side. This was only a theory, and before long he decided it was incorrect. Then he introduced a second theory, saying that dyslexia was 'mixed hemispheric dominance'. This meant that *sometimes* the right side of the brain was doing what the left side was supposed to, and vice-versa.

Today there are many different theories of what dyslexia is and what causes it. Most were formulated to explain the symptoms or characteristics of dyslexia—and why the disability occurred.

A NEW PERSPECTIVE

The theories and procedures in this book were developed not to explain the nature of the problem, but to explain *why it could be corrected*. The theories were developed during and after the development of the corrective procedures described in the final chapters. Because I used 'hindsight', and because I have first-hand experience at being a dyslexic, mine is an entirely different perspective.

This is what I've found out: dyslexia is not the result of brain damage or nerve damage. Nor is it caused by a malformation of the brain, inner ear or eyeballs. Dyslexia is a product of thought and a special way of reacting to the feeling of confusion.

TWO KINDS OF THOUGHT

It is widely believed that human beings think in two different ways: 'verbal conceptualisation' and 'non-verbal conceptualisation'.

Verbal conceptualisation means thinking with the *sounds* of words. Non-verbal conceptualisation means thinking with mental *pictures* of concepts or ideas.

Verbal thought is linear in time. It follows the structure of language. When using it, a person composes mental sentences one word at a time. Verbal thinking occurs at about the same speed as speech. Normal speech has a speed of about 150 words per minute, or 2.5 words per second.

A skilled radio announcer or auctioneer can race along at 200 words per minute. Electronically doctored speech can remain intelligible to an attentive listener at speeds of up to 250 words per minute. This is essentially the maximum limit of verbal conceptualisation.

Non-verbal thought is evolutionary. The picture 'grows' as the thought process adds more concepts. Non-verbal thought is much faster, possibly thousands of times faster. In fact, it's difficult to understand the non-verbal thinking process because it happens so fast you aren't aware of it when you do it. Usually non-verbal thinking is subliminal, or below conscious awareness.

People think in both verbal and non-verbal modes, but being human, we have a tendency to specialise. Each person will practise one mode as his or her primary mode of thinking and the other as a secondary mode.

During the period when the learning disability aspect of dyslexia is formed, between the ages of three and thirteen, the potential dyslexic must be primarily a non-verbal thinker—a person who thinks in pictures.

To see how this mode of thinking contributes to the dyslexic's learning disability, we must look at our language. We can consider language a mirror of the thought process. Otherwise language would be far too complicated for anyone to learn.

Language is composed of symbols. Symbols are composed of three parts:

1 What the symbol sounds like.

2 What the symbol means.

3 What the symbol looks like.

When we use verbal conceptualisation, we are thinking with the *sounds* of the language. We are actually carrying on an internal monologue of mental statements, questions and answers. Some people verbalise these conceptualisations by talking to themselves out loud. It's a slow process, but one that can make the meaning of a sentence easy to get, even though some of the words may not be fully understood.

Listening to a sentence mentally can aid understanding, because usually the symbols (letters and words) don't all occur in a sequence that makes the meaning of the sentence unfold as it is being read. For instance, you can't tell whether an English sentence is a statement or a question until you get to the end and discover whether it is followed by a full stop or a question mark—can you?

If we use non-verbal conceptualisation, we are thinking with the meaning of the language by forming mental pictures of its concepts and ideas. These pictures aren't just visual. They are more like three-dimensional, multisensory films. They change and evolve as a sentence is read. The process is many times faster than verbal conceptualisation. But it does present a problem, because some parts of the language are easier to picture as concepts and ideas than others are.

Keep in mind that dyslexics have little or no internal monologue, so they do not *hear* what they are reading unless they are reading aloud. Instead, they are composing a mental picture by adding the meaning—or image of the meaning—of each new word as it is encountered.

TWO KINDS OF WORDS

Words that describe real things don't cause dyslexics much trouble.

In non-verbal thought, we can think with the

word *elephant* easily if we know what an elephant looks like. The animal we call an 'elephant' is the literal meaning of the word *elephant*. Seeing its picture is seeing its meaning. We can think with the word *home* if we can picture a place where we once lived. We can think with nouns like *school*, *book*, *paper* and *pencil* so long as we know what they look like. We can think with verbs like *fly*, *sleep*, *view* and the like, because we have seen or experienced the actions the words describe.

It is impossible for a non-verbal thinker to think with words whose meanings can't be pictured. Knowing what an *a* looks like doesn't let us think with an *a*. Nor does knowing what an *and* or a *the* looks like allow us to think with those words. Seeing the letters *T-H-E* for the word *the* is not seeing its meaning. The only picture available is the forms of the letters themselves. When we use the picturing process of non-verbal thinking, we are not able to picture the meaning of the word as an object or an action.

If we read a sentence while using verbal conceptualisation, seeing words like *a*, *and* and *the* won't create a problem, because we know how they sound. We will create a picture of the meaning of a sentence only after we have completed reading the sentence. Even if we don't know the exact meanings of these words, we won't have a problem, because the overall idea of the sentence will be understood after we finish reading it and listen to it mentally.

Reading the same sentence while using non-verbal conceptualisation will produce dyslexic symptoms. The picture of the sentence's meaning is evolving as we read. The evolutionary development of the picture being formed by the sentence is stopped each time the meaning of an unknown word cannot be incorporated into the overall picture. The problem will be compounded every time we come across a word whose meaning does not have a corresponding mental picture. We end up with a series of unrelated pictures with blank spots in between.

In non-verbal conceptualisation, each time the picture-making process is stopped, the person will experience a feeling of confusion because the picture being composed becomes more incoherent. Using concentration, the reader can push past the blanks and continue, but will feel more and more confused the farther he goes. Eventually he will reach his *threshold of confusion*.

At this point, the person becomes *disorientated*. *Disorientation* means that perception of the symbols gets altered and becomes distorted so that reading or writing is difficult or impossible. Ironically, this shifting of perception is the exact mechanism that dyslexics have found useful for recognising real-life objects and events in their environment before they began learning to read.

CHAPTER 3

Effects of Disorientation

Orientation means knowing where you are in relation to your environment. In terms of perception, it means finding out the facts and conditions of your surroundings and putting yourself in the proper relation to them. When you see, hear and sense the outside world from a particular viewpoint that makes sense to you, you are orientated. An aeroplane or ship navigator has the job of determining the orientation of a plane or ship to its environment.

Humans orientate themselves visually by looking at the world through two eyes. The brain compares the two images the eyes see and uses the difference between them to form a three-dimensional mental image that tells us how far away things are. The ears do the same thing to determine from which direction a sound is coming. This technique is known as triangulation. It works the same way in perception as in navigation.

The exact point from which you perceive visually

is not on the lenses of your eyes, because those are two different points. It is actually a mental 'screen' in the brain. People generally have the impression that they are looking out at the world from somewhere behind their eyes.

THE MIND'S EYE

There is also a *mental* perception point from which a person looks at mental images and thoughts. If you close your eyes and look at an imaginary mental picture, this point of perception is where you are looking from, or what you are using in order to look. It is not the same as the visual perception point, but works on the same basic princple as vision: something is looking at something else. This 'epicentre of perception' is what I call 'the mind's eye'. When it shifts, it causes all the physical perceptions to disorientate. This is fully explained in Chapters 23 and 24. For the moment, let's just get an idea of what disorientation is and what it feels like.

Disorientation is a common occurrence. With very few exceptions, it happens to everyone at times. Disorientation is the natural function of a normal brain. It occurs when we are overwhelmed by stimuli or thought. It also occurs when the brain receives conflicting information from the different senses and attempts to correlate the information.

If you stand up and spin round quickly ten times, you will experience disorientation in the form of dizziness. If you stare at a spinning disc with a spiral painted on it, you will experience disorientation in the form of perceived movement. If you sit in your car at a red traffic light and the car ahead of you rolls backwards, you are likely to get the physical sensation that your own car is moving forward and press harder on the brake before you even think about it.

During a disorientation, your brain sees things moving that really aren't, or your body feels as if you are moving when you really aren't. Your sense of time can slow down or speed up. Your brain alters your actual perceptions, and you experience the altered perceptions as reality.

Whenever disorientation occurs, all the senses (except the sense of taste) are altered. The brain is no longer seeing what the eyes are seeing, but an altered perception of the images. The brain is no longer hearing what the ears are hearing, but an altered perception of the sounds. And so on through the rest of the perceptions, including the senses of touch, balance, motion and time.

THE DYSLEXIC DILEMMA

While disorientation is a common experience, dyslexics have taken it far beyond the ordinary. They

A Clue About Disorientation

During my first year of college, I got a bad cold that developed into a severe inner ear infection. I lay delirious in hospital for two days, then woke up experiencing uncontrollable disorientation. Sounds were so loud they were painful to hear. I saw multiple images. My fingers wouldn't do what I wanted them to do. When I opened my eyes, **all** *my senses told me I was spinning in space.*

When I asked the doctor what was happening, he told me that it was because my brain was receiving and sending conflicting sensory perceptions.

'Your inner ears have two organs that tell your brain which way is up,' he explained. 'The right one is working, but the left one is telling your brain that **up** *is some other direction. The two signals don't agree, so you feel as if you're spinning round.'*

'But I can **see** *that I'm spinning,' I said. 'Why is that?'*

'Your senses aren't allowed to disagree,' said the doctor. 'It seems to be the way the brain is constructed. Your vision is adjusting to make the signals agree with each other. The spinning you see is tracking with the distortions in your sense of balance.'

At the time, it helped to know that what I was experiencing was a result of the illness, and that the distortions would go away. Later on, when I began researching disorientation, this clue stuck in my mind. It explained why a distortion of one perception causes the others to shift correspondingly.

don't just experience disorientation, they cause it to occur without realising it.

Dyslexics use disorientation on an unconscious level in order to perceive multidimensionally. By shifting their senses, they are able to experience multiple views of the world. They can perceive things from more than one perspective and gain more information from these perceptions than other people.

Apparently, as infants they somehow found a way to access the disorientation function of the brain and incorporated it into their thought and recognition processes. For infants who can't easily move about to examine things, being able to 'fill in the blanks' and see things mentally from more than one perspective comes in handy.

Because the altered perceptions bring about recognition of objects that would otherwise be unrecognisable, disorientation becomes a normal part of their thinking process. Dyslexics are not aware of what occurs during the disorientation because it happens too fast. They are only aware of what occurs when they use it: better recognition of three-dimensional objects, sounds and tactile stimuli. Besides resolving confusion, dyslexics utilise the altered perceptions that occur with disorientations for creative imagination. When it is applied to solving a problem during non-verbal conceptualisation, it might be called intuition, invention or inspiration. When it is done for entertainment, it is called fantasising or daydreaming.

More about the inherent *talents* of dyslexics will be covered later. For the moment, it is enough to say that incorporating disorientation into the thought process can make dyslexics more perceptive or imaginative than the average person. When they begin to use language, it also creates the potential for developing a learning disability.

Until now, the dyslexic has been using disorientation to *resolve* confusion. This worked very well when dealing with real physical objects, so the dyslexic is likely to disorientate unconsciously when a confusing symbol is encountered. Unfortunately, viewing a printed word on a page from the top or the back, or scrambled into its component parts, makes the word more confusing than ever.

While learning to read, as confusions pile up, dyslexics will quickly reach their threshold of confusion. At this point, the dyslexic is no longer seeing what is actually written on the page, but what he or she *thinks* is on the page. Because the symbol isn't an object, and only represents the sound of a word that describes an object, action or idea, disorientation won't aid in its recognition. Because the symbol isn't recognised, the dyslexic will make a mistake. These mistakes are the primary symptoms of dyslexia.

CHAPTER 4

Dyslexia in Action

There are more than 200 English words that cause problems for most dyslexics. They are in the dyslexic's speaking vocabulary, but the dyslexic cannot form mental pictures of their meanings. That means the average dyslexic uses more than two hundred words in speech with which he or she cannot really think. These little words—seemingly the most simple words in the language—are the stimuli or triggers for the symptoms of dyslexia.

Trigger words have abstract meanings, and often a number of different meanings. They trip up dyslexics because they do not represent visual objects or actions. They also happen to be the words which occur most frequently in everyday speech and writing. A complete list of trigger words is in Chapter 33.

Origin of the Trigger Word List

I didn't invent this list. Like so many other discoveries related to my work, it came with a degree of surprise and the thought, 'It's so obvious, I should have known it all along.'

Soon after making my initial discovery about perception, it became apparent that confusion triggered disorientations, and that confusion occurred whenever the person did not recognise a symbol. I thought each dyslexic would have a small, unique list of trigger words. Our programmes included teaching students to notice disorientations when they occurred and to compile a list of their trigger words, so that they would know which words to master.

As I began making my own list, I was surprised. It wasn't at all what I had thought it would be. I was embarrassed that it contained both of the one-letter words, all of the two-letter words, and mostly four-letter words. I felt a little better when the lists made by our clients contained the same words, but I still wondered why.

One evening in August 1982, I was looking over the list of basic sight words used by primary school teachers. I checked off a few words and pondered why some (such as a, *and* and *the) triggered disorientations, and others (such as* home, food *and* friend) *didn't trigger dyslexic symptoms. I began carefully to examine my mental processes as I read each word. As in a cartoon where the light bulb goes on above a head, my realisation lit up my universe. I discovered that I had no mental pictures for the trigger words. I couldn't picture them, so I couldn't think with them.*

From the basic list I was able to identify 196 words that trigger disorientation. Today, the list has grown to 217 words. Most of the additions are contractions or other forms of words from the original list.

HOW TRIGGER WORDS CAUSE PROBLEMS

To put the puzzle pieces together, let's look at a typical scenario of a dyslexic child trying to read aloud.

A simple sentence like the one below would be easy to read for a ten-year-old who thinks with the sounds of words. But for a ten-year-old dyslexic who constructs mental pictures of the scene as each word is read, the process is more difficult.

> *The brown horse jumped over the stone*
> *wall and ran through the pasture.*

For the ten-year-old dyslexic, the first word, *The*, caused the mental imagery to go blank, because there was no picture for it. A blank picture is the essence of confusion; nothing a person experiences can match the confusion it causes. Using concentration, however, the child pushes past the blank picture and says 'the', and forces himself to skip to the next word.

The word *brown* produces a mental image of a colour, but it has no defined shape. Continuing to concentrate, he says 'brown'.

The word *horse* transforms the brown picture into a horse of that colour. Concentration continues and 'horse' is said.

The word *jumped* causes the front of the brown horse to rise into the air. He continues concentrating as he says 'jumped'.

The word *over* causes the back of the brown horse to rise. Still concentrating, he says 'over'.

The next word, another *the*, causes the picture to go blank again. Confusion for the reader has increased, but the threshold of confusion has not yet been reached. He must now double his concentration so that he can push on to the next word. In doing so, he may or may not omit saying 'the'.

The word *stone* produces a picture of a rock. With concentration doubled, he says 'stone'.

The next word, *wall*, turns the rock into a rock wall. Still with doubled concentration, he says 'wall'.

The next word, *and*, blanks out the picture again. This time, the threshold for confusion is reached. So the child becomes disorientated. The child is stopped again, more confused, doubly concentrating, and now disorientated. The only way he can continue is to increase his concentration effort. But now because he is also disorientated, the dyslexic symptoms will appear. It is very likely that he will omit saying the word 'and', or just as likely that he will substitute 'a', 'an' or 'the' instead. At this point, he is no longer getting an accurate perception of the words on the page.

He is now expending a tremendous amount of effort and energy on concentrating, just to continue.

The next word, *ran*, because he is now disorientated, is altered into the word *runs*. He sees an image of himself running, entirely unrelated to the picture of the hovering horse. Then he says 'runs'.

The word *through* is altered into *throws*. He sees himself throwing a ball and says 'throws'.

The next word, *the*, blanks out the picture again. The child is stopped again, even more confused, and still disorientated. His only recourse is to quadruple his concentration. In doing so, he omits saying 'the'.

By now his disorientation has created a feeling like dizziness. He is feeling sick and the words and letters are swimming around on the page.

For the last word, *pasture*, he must track down each letter, one at a time, so he can sound out the word. Once he does, he sees a picture of a grassy place. Even though he is disorientated, because of the extra effort and energy he put forth in catching and sounding out each letter, he says it right, 'pasture'.

Having completed the sentence, he closes the book and pushes it away. That's enough of that!

When asked what he has just read, he is likely to answer with something like 'a place where grass grows.' He has a picture of a horse in the air, a stone wall, himself playing ball and a grassy place, but cannot relate the separate elements in the sentence to form a mental image of the scene described.

To everyone who saw or heard him read the sentence or heard his answer to what it was about, it's obvious that he didn't understand any of what he just read. As for him, he doesn't care that he didn't

Word	Reaction	Sees/thinks	Says
The	picturing process stops; concentration begins	blank picture	*the*
brown	concentration continues	brown colour	*brown*
horse	concentration continues	brown horse	*horse*
jumped	concentration continues	front of the horse rises	*jumped*
over	concentration continues	back of horse rises	*over*
the	picturing process stops; concentration doubles	blank picture	*the*
stone	doubled concentration	a rock	*stone*
wall	doubled concentration	rock wall	*wall*
and	picturing process stops; disorientation occurs; concentration triples	blank picture	*(omits word?)*
ran	disorientation continues; tripled concentration	running	*runs*
through	disorientation continues; tripled concentration	throwing a ball	*throws*
the	picturing process stops; disorientation continues; concentration quadruples	blank picture	*(omits word)*
pasture	disorientation continues; quadrupled concentration	a grassy place	*pasture*

understand it. He's just thankful that he survived the ordeal of reading aloud.

If he were a little older he would realise that he has just read something that he didn't understand. So what would he probably do? *Read it again.* It seems logical that if we read it again we'll get more out of it—doesn't it? Look again at the scenario above and ask the question, 'What has changed that will make reading the sentence any different the second time?' *Nothing!*

When reading important or technical data, adult dyslexics will reread the material between three and ten times before they feel they understand it, or they will abandon the attempt.

ISN'T CONCENTRATION GOOD?

I should clarify a point here about concentration: Most people consider it a positive ability, but too much of anything, even something positive, can be detrimental. The degree to which the dyslexic must concentrate to push past a blank picture definitely produces a negative effect.

When people concentrate on something, they are putting most of their awareness on that thing. When they are intensely concentrating, they are *limiting* their awareness to that thing *alone*.

This is a fundamental aspect of hypnotism. It is the

exact mechanism used by hypnotists to put someone into a trance. When dyslexics concentrate intensely in order to read, they experience a hypnotic state which adds to the difficulty of understanding the material read, as well as the time required to comprehend it.

CHAPTER 5

Compulsive Solutions

Once disorientations begin to cause mistakes, the dyslexic child becomes frustrated. Nobody likes to make mistakes, so around the age of nine, in his or her fifth year at school, the dyslexic child begins to find, work out and adopt solutions to the problem. Even though this may seem a good thing, it is actually how the reading problem becomes a true learning disability.

The solutions dyslexics invent don't solve the real problem of distorted perceptions; they only afford temporary relief from frustrations. They are roundabout methods of coping with the effects of disorientation that ultimately slow down the learning process and form the real learning disability.

These 'solutions' are methods of doing things or tactics for knowing or remembering things. They quickly become compulsive behaviours. Once a dyslexic adopts one, it will be the only way she can perform that particular function. During the process of correcting dyslexia, I refer to these as 'old solutions', because they are no longer needed.

Although many dyslexics begin developing compulsive solutions before the age of nine, and continue to develop more for the rest of their lives, most of these 'learning crutches' are developed between the ages of nine and twelve. Dyslexics usually have hundreds if not thousands of them.

Here are a few common examples of compulsive solutions.

THE ALPHABET SONG

A common childhood solution is reciting the Alphabet Song. If the song is learned at home or at school as a simple training pattern, within two years most children will be able to recite the alphabet without either singing the song or replaying it mentally. But if a child adopts the song as a solution to being unable to learn the alphabet, she will never be able to recite the alphabet without either singing it out loud or replaying it mentally.

She only knows the song; the song knows the alphabet. So by using the song, she can *appear* to know the alphabet. Whenever she wants to look up a name in the phone book or a word in the dictionary, the song will be used. It has become a compulsive behaviour.

HEAVY CONCENTRATION

Of all the compulsive solutions dyslexics come up with, probably the worst one is 'concentration'. Before learning how to concentrate, most dyslexics can't read at all. Once they learn to concentrate hard enough, they do learn how to read—slowly and laboriously. The problem is that reading will be unpleasant and painful for them. If what they are trying to read is important, they will have to read it over and over many times to make sure it's correct. They won't read for pleasure, because there is no pleasure in heavy concentration.

Probably the most common characteristics of dyslexia in adults are slow reading, going over the same material many times and tension headaches caused by the heavy concentration they use to read.

There is a clear distinction with dyslexics between concentration and *paying attention*. Paying attention to something interesting is fun. Concentration on something life-threatening is no fun at all. In fact, it is highly stressful. The inability to read and write often seems life-threatening to a dyslexic person.

'DO IT FOR ME'

For adult dyslexics, an easier solution than heavy concentration is getting other people to read and write things for them. You may have been tricked into doing this by someone who said, 'Would you read this and tell me what you think of it?'

Do you remember how that person fished for more information? It was a ploy, even though you probably didn't notice. Your opinion really wasn't what he was after; it was the information contained in whatever you were asked to read. Your reading skills were utilised by a dyslexic who couldn't decipher the words on the page and got you to interpret them.

Some brilliant dyslexics become corporate executives because of their intuitive gifts for 'seeing' the correct strategy and mobilising the work force. They will always invest heavily in the latest dictation and video equipment—anything that transmits information in a form other than writing. They will rely on trusted subordinates to read things for them and relay messages that must be delivered in writing. That's because they are secretly functional illiterates.

FOR BETTER OR FOR WORSE?

It is ironic that many of the 'best' teaching and tutoring techniques used to help dyslexics do nothing more than implant and reinforce compulsive behaviours. This is understandable, because it appears the dyslexic is finally beginning to learn.

This is only an illusion. The child is actually being conditioned into performing rote acts that aren't really understood. This conditioning will be a lifetime disability unless it is corrected at some point in the future.

CHAPTER 6

Problems With Reading

(Especially English)

You may have forgotten what it was like to learn to read. Most people who can read fairly well do it automatically, unaware of how many gyrations their minds are going through. Reading is considered by many researchers to be the most complex function we require our brains to perform.

Maybe you have heard about computer software that performs optical character recognition. It 'reads' an image of printing and converts it into text characters that can be used in a computer program. The Post Office uses it to read typed postcodes for mail sorting. These programs take a long time to work as they crawl along, letter by letter. They also tend to make many mistakes. It's a wonder they work at all, considering the complexity of what they have to do.

When you read, your brain has to do the same thing (though you probably recognise many entire words). Then you have to look up the words in your mental dictionary and string them together so that they make sense within the context of a complete sentence or thought. You are actually converting characters into word sounds, then combining those words into speech. For a dyslexic, this poses two problems.

First, when disorientated, a dyslexic's optical character recognition software isn't getting a clear picture of the characters on the page—it's trying to read the equivalent of a poor copy, so it makes more mistakes.

Secondly, a dyslexic doesn't really 'hear' thoughts internally. This means that she doesn't mentally sound out the words as she reads. In fact, despite the popularity of phonic methods to teach reading, dyslexics usually do better at sight reading, where they simply recognise an individual word as a concept.

The problems dyslexics have in learning to read are the same as those all children experience, but of a larger magnitude. They are made worse by inconsistencies in the language. If the printed word were presented more consistently, especially in primary schoolbooks, some of these problems would be lessened for all children.

THE PROBLEM WITH TYPOGRAPHY

Until after the turn of the century, all printing looked pretty similar. This was because when text was prepared for printing, typographers used characters made from metal castings. A printer could only afford so many sets of type, and they had to fit together uniformly in a row. The main exception was hand-painted signs and posters.

Today, thanks to computerised typesetting, we have a wealth of styles to choose from. Graphic designers can express themselves even further by warping, bending and otherwise distorting type styles. This makes the printed page look more artistic but less legible, especially to dyslexics who are adding distortions of their own every time they come across a word or symbol that makes them disorientate.

This is true even of dictionaries used by school children. For example, here are the beginnings of three entries from a 'young people's' dictionary. What do you think they say?

III

I'll

III.

Here are the complete entries:

III   a Roman numeral for the figure 3.

I'll   1. I shall. 2. I will.

III.   abbreviation for Illinois.

Note that you cannot really tell whether or not the

abbreviation for Illinois is the Roman numeral three, since either one would normally be followed by a period; nor is it possible to distinguish the capital 'I' from the lower-case 'L'.

Here are a few examples of different type styles. As an experiment, try turning this book upside down or hold it in front of a mirror and see which ones are harder to read. You'll probably find that those which give you the most trouble are the most unusual ones, or those with the most complex decorative elements. Those are the typefaces that tend to give dyslexics the most trouble.

ABCDEFGHIJKLMNOPQRSTUVWXYZ
zyxwvutsrqponmlkjihgfedcba   1234567890

ABCDEFGHIJKLMNOPQRSTUVWXYZ
ZYXWVUTSRQPONMLKJIHGFEDCBA   1234567890

ABCDEFGHIJKLMNOPQRSTUVWXYZ
zyxwvutsrqponmlkjihgfedcba   1234567890

ABCDEFGHIJKLMNOPQRSTUVWXYZ
ZYXWVUTSRQPONMLKJIHGFEDCBA   1234567890

𝕬𝕭𝕮𝕯𝕰𝕱𝕲𝕳𝕴𝕵𝕶𝕷𝕸𝕹𝕺𝕻𝕼𝕽𝕾𝕿𝖀𝖁𝖂𝖃𝖄𝖅
zyxwvutsrqponmlkjihgfedcba   1234567890

ABCDEFGHIJKLMNOPQRSTUVWXYZ
zyxwvutsrqponmlkjihgfedcba   1234567890

ABCDEFGHIJKLMNOPQRSTUVWXYZ
zyxwvutsrqponmlkjihgfedcba   1234567890

ABCDEFGHIJKLMNOPQRSTUVWXYZ
zyxwvutsrqponmlkjihgfedcba   1234567890

ABCDEFGHIJKLMNOPQRSTUVWXYZ
zyxwvutsrqponmlkjihgfedcba   1234567890

ABCDEFGHIJKLMNOPQRSTUVWXYZ
zyxwvutsrqponmlkjihgfedcba 1234567890

ALPHABETICAL OBSTACLES

Our alphabet is not phonetically accurate. In order to represent all the possible sounds of speech, it would need about 44 characters. The Russian alphabet, for instance, has 32 characters, not 26. Some languages have 50 characters or more. This eliminates the need for some characters or combinations of characters to represent as many as five different sounds, as they do in English. If you read aloud in some languages and simply pronounce the letters phonetically, you will say every word correctly without guessing about the sounds you are supposed to make.

Even other languages that use the same characters as English, such as Spanish, French and Portuguese, make liberal use of accents over certain letters, like *a* and *e*, to help people pronounce them accurately.

The Spanish are polite enough to warn us beforehand that a sentence is going to be a question by putting an upside-down question mark at the beginning.

Naturally, dyslexia is a worldwide phenomenon, at least wherever languages are made up of sound symbols. The possible exception may be languages that use pictographs, such as Chinese. The variations in cultures and teaching methods would make it difficult to discern the exact influence of different languages on the learning process. But common sense tells me that English, with its multitude of inconsistencies, is one of the more difficult languages for dyslexics to pronounce and spell correctly.

It might help if teachers explained to students that our language is a rather messy system, with so many variations and exceptions to the rules that the rules often don't work at all.

Reading is not the only place where dyslexia symptoms show up. Because dyslexics naturally respond to confusion by becoming disorientated, wherever we find symbols—spoken or written—we can find symptoms. The most common areas are spelling, maths, handwriting, attention deficits and hyperactivity.

CHAPTER 7

Spelling Problems

The spelling problems dyslexics have are mostly the result of disorientation. When a disorientation occurs, the person gets multiple views of the word. Not only is it looked at forwards, backwards and upside down both ways, it is pulled apart and reassembled in every possible combination. There are at least forty different variations of a three-letter word such as 'cat', and only six of these are 'logical' versions, with the letters in their correct configurations (*see illustration on page 86*).

These variations, of course, only involve rearranging the letters two-dimensionally. Dyslexics often see the letters three-dimensionally, as if they were floating in space. This creates an infinite number of different views. One little girl said they crawled off the page and hid in the carpet.

THE RULES DON'T WORK

Teaching the student spelling rules is frustrating, because there are so many exceptions to the rules. One out of six words is phonetically irregular. If you teach a corrected dyslexic the rules, his spelling scores may actually go down. This is because when spelling is tested, it is usually to see whether the person knows the exceptions to the rules. If he follows the rules strictly, the test will be a disaster.

Once perception is accurate, spelling improvement will follow. Symbol Mastery (Chapters 31 and 33) and Spell-Reading (Chapter 32) are the best methods I have discovered for teaching dyslexics to recognise and spell words they will need to use in everyday reading and writing.

A written word is nothing more than a symbol composed of one or more alphabet symbols. The symbols together indicate what it looks like (on paper), what it sounds like (when someone says it), and what it means. Spelling is only the 'what it looks like' component. When the word is mastered using Symbol Mastery, the person learns all three parts, and can utilise the word fully in reading, speaking and thinking.

HOW IMPORTANT IS IT?

Our educational system has an obsession with accuracy in spelling. It wasn't always so. In Elizabethan England, many variations were acceptable so long as people could understand how the word was supposed to sound. Spelling styles have changed considerably over the years, as you can tell by looking at a facsimile of an original Shakespeare play. How do you think William Shakespeare would do in a spelling test today?

Instead of turning spelling into a contest, it's better simply to point out the difference between the word the student wrote and the correct spelling (or spellings) in the dictionary. Eventually, corrected dyslexics will work out on their own how to spell the words as they read. As improvement occurs, it is important not to criticise students or make them feel wrong for making errors.

If a student continues to make spelling mistakes by attempting to spell words phonetically, blame it on our imprecise system of phonetics, not on the student.

CHAPTER 8

Maths Problems

Not all dyslexics have problems with maths. When they do, it is usually called *acalculia* or *dyscalculia*. Many common difficulties with maths result from the methods that are used in attempting to teach it. But the dyslexic has an underlying problem that can make learning maths difficult, if not impossible.

Acalculia and dyscalculia can be traced directly to the time-sense distortions that are common among dyslexic children. They occur simultaneously with visual and auditory disorientations.

THE MENTAL TIME CLOCK

Everyone experiences time-sense distortion to some degree. It is usually related to the emotions of boredom and excitement. When you become bored, your internal clock speeds up, and time seems to drag. When you become excited, your internal clock slows down, and time seems to fly by. These distortions are minor compared to those a dyslexic experiences during periods of disorientation. If the dyslexic is a dancer, athlete or fireman, the ability to experience time in slow motion can be a great advantage. This is why some dancers and football players are able to give the appearance of 'hovering in mid-air'.

I have a theory that, biochemically, a person's time sense is primarily controlled by the amount of the neurotransmitter dopamine around the synapses of the brain. The more dopamine, the faster the internal clock goes. The faster it goes, the more external time seems to slow down. The less dopamine, the slower the clock goes. External time seems to speed up. Disorientations seem to cause a change in the amount of dopamine that is created and dispersed in the brain.

Disorientation is a constant mental companion to dyslexic children. As they go through childhood, distorted perception is as common as actual perception. Because of this, most dyslexic children have little sense of time. Ordinary children experience time rather consistently. By the age of seven, they can estimate the passage of time with fair accuracy. For the dyslexic, time has never been consistently experienced, so estimating its passage may be impossible.

Without an inherent sense of time, understanding the concept of *sequence*—the way things follow each other, one after another—would be difficult if not impossible. Even simple counting is a matter of sequence. So the seven-year-old dyslexic could also lack this inherent concept.

Without the concepts of time and sequence, an accurate understanding of the concept of 'order versus disorder' is doubtful.

THE BASICS OF MATHS

All maths, from simple arithmetic to astrophysics calculus, is composed of order (versus disorder), sequence and time. Children who have an inherent sense of these three concepts can learn and understand maths. For children who do not possess these concepts, learning maths is reduced to memorisation. The extent to which they will be able to use maths is limited by their ability to remember the rote procedures. Without an understanding of these underlying concepts, there will never be any real understanding of the subject or its principles.

For a dyslexic to learn maths, the basics must be mastered:

1 *Time*, meaning the measurement of change in relation to a standard.

2 *Sequence*, meaning the way things follow each other, one after another in amount, in size, in time or in importance.

3   *Order*, meaning things in their proper places, proper positions and proper conditions.

Once these concepts are mastered, accurate counting can be mastered. Then learning arithmetic may change from a labour to a joy.

An interesting side-note is that mathematics and music are composed of the same three elements: order, sequence and time. They are just expressed in different media. So it shouldn't be surprising that many top mathematicians are also excellent musicians, and vice-versa.

CHAPTER 9

Handwriting Problems

When a dyslexic has a writing problem, it is usually diagnosed as *agraphia* or *dysgraphia*. It is related to disorientation. There are several reasons for writing problems. Sometimes poor writing is used to cover up spelling problems or other deficiencies. Sometimes it is simply because writing instructions were given while the dyslexic was disorientated.

MULTIPLE MENTAL PICTURES

The most common type of writing problem occurs when dyslexic students have had so much instruction on what their writing *should* look like that they have multiple mental pictures of words and letters superimposed over one another. With a pen or pencil they can only make one line at a time, so what they draw is a combination of all of these pictures, usually switching from one to another. The result is a jumble of lines that wiggle and jump all over the paper.

The solution is to get rid of all the old mental pictures. Once the pictures are gone, the student can see a clear, single mental picture of what writing should look like. In these cases, it is fortunate that dyslexics have such vivid mental images. By following the simple procedure of having the person access and erase the superfluous pictures one by one, it is easy to eliminate them.

DORMANT NEURAL PATHWAYS

The worst type of writing problem is the most difficult to explain because of the biophysics by which the brain processes stimuli and produces function.

Picture the brain as a large fishing net. There are vertical cords and horizontal cords, and wherever the cords cross there is a knot. In this model, the cords would be neurons and the knots would be synapses. By tracing along the cords, you can move from any knot to any other knot in the net. So theoretically every synapse of the brain is connected to every other synapse.

Add to the picture that the net is divided into several hundred different areas, and each area provides a different service to the whole. There are seeing areas, hearing areas, finger-wiggling areas, and so on for everything humans can perceive and do.

As a perceptual stimulus comes into the net, the first knot is stimulated. From there the signal is processed by sending other stimuli along other cords to other knots, and so on, until the original stimulus has reached all the knots it must reach. There is an untold number of different paths which this stimulus could follow, but once a particular path is used, it becomes stronger. The stronger it is, the more it is used. Also, there are certain paths that are never stimulated, so they remain weak and unused.

Consider that the paths are neural pathways, and that as a unit they form a neural network. Now consider that because of a dyslexic's distorted perceptions (disorientation), the neural pathway for seeing straight diagonal lines has never been stimulated. This person would simply not be able to see straight diagonal lines.

This isn't to say that the person's eyes wouldn't pass along the images correctly. The problem is that the brain wouldn't process diagonal line images. The neural pathways for processing the stimuli have never been used. Also, because the brain has never been able to see a straight diagonal line, it cannot instruct the hand to draw one, because the neural pathway for making one has never been used.

Because a dysgraphic child must make straight diagonal lines in writing, but has never seen one, the child will draw what he or she saw. The distorted perception that was formed when looking at straight

May 14

"See whar I DiD?" (Sade) Andy.
I ush you! , is that a Drawing
you Bo, it is (Sade) Bety
When. see, saw it.
Yes, it is (Sade) Joe.
It has a lot in it
come on

May 16

Agenst the bakground I can tell
you the absolutly the best
flit I ever made never left
inside a brick bilding at
Kennedy Airport.
It was in TWA's 747 simulator.

May 17

I'm going to go all over. First I'm
going to Saint Louis for my family
reunion on my moms side. Then I'm
going to a neat camp up in Mendocino
called Camp Winarainbow. After that
I might go to Idaho to visit my
uncle.

Handwriting samples made by an 11-year-old boy with agraphia during the Davis Orientation Counselling Programme.

'How did you do that?'

We're often asked how the changes in handwriting illustrated here could have occurred in only four days.

This boy had a genius IQ. At the age of eleven he was reading the encyclopedia for pleasure, and dictating full-length plays and short novels to his mother. Each time he tried to write, however, he would break the pencil lead after only a few words. His primary goal was to overcome his agraphia and learn to write cursively.

The underlying cause of his agraphia was a combination of strong disorientations in the senses of vision and motion, multiple mental pictures of what written words should look like, and undeveloped neural pathways for seeing certain types or attitudes of lines.

The first step in correcting his agraphia was Orientation Counselling. Then he completed Alphabet and Punctuation Mastery as described in Chapter 31.

Another step in addressing his handwriting problem was to give him a sample of each letter and ask him to copy it. Those he could not write required motions that triggered disorientations. Once these were located, each motion was practised one at a time, first in space and then very large on paper, until they no longer triggered disorientations. These included many of the loops and changes in direction used in cursive writing.

His pencil grip was addressed by having him practise large drawing motions with a marker on a large piece of paper. The size was gradually decreased until he could use a pencil or pen on a piece of paper to make small marks and doodles.

Finally he practised writing a word. After each attempt, he was asked if he had any mental pictures of what that word should look like and was told to erase all the pictures. This was repeated until he no longer had a picture of what the word 'should' look like and had only a single picture. This procedure was repeated with many words, to a point where he spontaneously erased all his last pictures of 'what words should look like'. At that point, with simple penmanship instruction, he quickly learned to write.

diagonal lines will be the model for what the 'make the line' neural pathway will tell the hand to produce.

This is a simplistic model, but the principle is accurate. I have worked with many dyslexics who simply couldn't see diagonal lines. Using clay, they could not form letters with diagonal lines such as *A, M, N, W, V* and *X*. Usually *W* is the worst. These people just can't grasp how to attach four straight ropes of clay together to make them look like a *W*.

Sometimes when a mother or teacher is watching me work with such a student, she becomes frustrated because the student can't seem to make it happen. I don't get frustrated, because I know what is really happening.

Once the student is orientated, I know that the neural pathways for seeing straight diagonal lines can now be stimulated. They are no longer blocked because of distortions. I also know that the student is opening up previously unused neural pathways at each attempt to put the pieces of clay together. It doesn't take long, usually less than an hour, before the pathway is opened and the student creates a diagonal line. Once the pathway opens, it becomes stronger and stronger. Usually within a day or two, the student can see all the straight diagonal lines in the surrounding environment that have been invisible or distorted up to that point.

In the example, I used straight diagonal lines. In real life it is not limited to that. The same thing can happen with any number of visual stimuli. It is remedied by providing stimuli to the person in a correctly orientated condition, then having him create the missing information using Symbol Mastery.

CHAPTER 10

The Newest Disability: ADD

The main thing new about *attention deficit disorder*, or ADD, is the use of these words to describe a learning disability. The problem has been around ever since teachers have attempted to teach students subjects that didn't interest them. In most cases, it should be described not as a learning disability, but as a teaching disability.

There is a genuine medical disorder called ADD which prevents a person from maintaining attention. It would certainly hinder performance in school if it were the real problem.

Currently, many students who cannot maintain fixed attention on a task for very long are being diagnosed as suffering from ADD. They are said to be 'easily distractible'. They shift their attention to other things in the environment instead of sticking to what the teacher has assigned.

Sometimes the ADD problem is accompanied by another condition called hyperactivity. Both are rooted in the developmental differences of dyslexic children during early childhood.

DIFFERENT LEARNING STYLES

'Normal' children bring to the classroom an underlying characteristic that dyslexic children lack. A child who isn't dyslexic has already begun to develop the ability to concentrate prior to starting school. A dyslexic child probably won't begin developing this questionable ability until about the age of nine.

Dyslexic children can assess and use the mental function of distorted perception to bring about recognition of objects and events in the environment. This is their natural, normal reaction to the feeling of confusion. When they use the distorted perception function, they achieve recognition and the feeling of confusion disappears. Because of this, most dyslexic children aren't well accustomed to the feeling of confusion. When it happens, it is almost instantly eliminated.

Other pre-school children go through periods of prolonged confusion, if for no other reason than their inability to eliminate it.

The feeling of confusion draws more and more attention to the source of the confusion. The end result of prolonged confusion is concentration, simply because most of the child's attention is being fixed upon whatever caused the confusion. Children who do not have a method of quickly eliminating confusion develop the ability to concentrate. Dyslexic children do not develop this ability at an early age because the stimuli for developing it can be eliminated so quickly and easily.

ATTENTION VS. CONCENTRATION

It is natural and easy for dyslexic children to pay attention, but difficult for them to concentrate. There is a tremendous difference between the two. When people are paying attention, their awareness is spread out; it can encompass the entire immediate environment. When people are concentrating, all or most of their attention is fixed on only one thing in the immediate environment.

My opinion is that heavy concentration produces a superficial, rote type of learning, characterised by memorisation without full understanding. Children who learn in this way can go through the motions, but don't fully grasp the underlying concepts of the subjects being taught.

While watching TV or playing with toys, the greater the child's interest or curiosity, the more attention the child will give to it. But there is still some attention left over for the rest of the environment. In other words, the child is paying more attention to one thing, but is still not abandoning or excluding the rest of the environment. This is true of ordinary children as well as dyslexics, but the dyslexic child will keep attention more widely spread around the environment than the ordinary child will.

CURIOSITY

Because dyslexic children are generally so environmentally aware, they tend to be curious. Curiosity, more than anything else, can cause them to shift their attention. If they find the object of curiosity interesting, they will pay more attention to it than to other things in the environment. They automatically give most of their attention to whatever they find most interesting.

If a dyslexic child sitting in a classroom hears a noise outside, or something moves past the window, or a student in the next row drops something, instantly the dyslexic's attention shifts to the distraction. The other students and possibly the teacher weren't even aware that anything happened. But the dyslexic student naturally reacted because he or she noticed it and became curious about what it might be.

Boredom also plays a role, because boredom often affects someone whose mind is working between four hundred and two thousand times faster than the minds of the people around him. A dyslexic child who is bored will do one of two things. Either the child will disorientate into creative imagination (daydreaming), or he will shift his attention to something else that *is* interesting (distractibility or inattention).

The impulsive aspect of ADD is most prevalent when the student is confused or uncertain about what to do. Otherwise, it is usually just an attempt to overcome agonising boredom.

There is a growing recognition that the symptoms of ADD, like those of dyslexia, can be an advantage in many real-life situations. During the past few years the potential benefits have been explored in a number of books on the subject. See Recommended References at the end of this book.

A highly regimented classroom is not a real-life situation by any strength of the imagination.

If the teacher does not appeal to the curiosity of a student and has failed to make the subject being taught the most interesting thing in the environment, the teacher has created the perfect environment for ADD. This teacher will eventually tell the parents of a dyslexic child that the child can't stay on task, is easily distractible, and should be assessed.

HYPERACTIVITY

When ADD is accompanied by hyperactivity it creates a bigger problem in the classroom, so the child is more likely to be singled out for diagnosis and treatment, often with Ritalin or other drugs. Hyperactivity is simply the addition of physical movement by the student.

Usually it is dyslexics who get tagged with the *hyper* label because of the physical effects of disorientation. Most students simply become bored and struggle to stay awake when they are uninterested or confused. Dyslexics also become disorientated.

The mechanism of hyperactivity is easy to understand when viewed from the following perspective. First the student isn't interested in what is going on, and doesn't understand what the teacher is saying. The resulting boredom and confusion activate the perception-altering function of the brain, and the student becomes disorientated. While bored, confused, and therefore disorientated, the student's internal clock speeds up, so perceived external time seems to slow down. For every minute of actual time, this student must endure two minutes of trying to stay out of trouble, pay attention, concentrate or sit still.

The student's senses are distorted, including the senses of balance and movement. The senses of balance and movement register in only two ways: you are either still or moving; you are either balanced or out of balance. If the student is sitting still when the distortions begin, he or she will have the sense of moving. If the student sits still long enough, motion sickness will set in. If the student begins to move, the sensations will reverse and the student will feel as if he or she is sitting still. This is why the student began to move around: to compensate for the feeling of motion sickness and keep from having an upset stomach or throwing up. This may be why Ritalin, a stimulant, works in reverse and seems to slow down 'hyperactive' schoolchildren.

Because the student's perceptions are distorted and the offensive movement is a product of these distorted perceptions, every time he or she is told to *sit still*, the movement will increase. This happens because the senses of balance and movement are reversed. If the student learned how to achieve orientation, the perception distortion function of the brain could be turned off. The student could perceive the environment accurately. The need to move to compensate for the distorted balance and movement perceptions would be gone.

Learning to become orientated stops the disorientation symptoms, but it will never make a student interested in a subject that is poorly taught. It is interesting that very good teachers rarely seem to have students with ADD in their classes, even though some of the same students are labelled as suffering from ADD in other classes.

CHAPTER 11

Clumsiness

Some dyslexics suffer from a particular type of chronic clumsiness called dyspraxia. It isn't always associated with dyslexia because it does not directly affect reading, writing, spelling or maths. It is one of the multiple facets of the gift of dyslexia.

It is likely that the phrase 'He can't walk and chew at the same time' was invented to describe a severely dyspraxic person. 'Accident prone' is another common term for dyspraxia in our culture. One mother told me her son *never grew out of his awkward stage*. When we consider distorted perception as the root of the problem, dyspraxia makes sense.

Dyspraxia has two causes. First, the senses of balance and movement are distorted because of disorientation. This is obvious, because disorientation can cause the sensation of dizziness. However, distortion in perception can occur even when someone is *not* disorientated. This is because that person's natural orientation is not optimum.

Even when the perceptions stop distorting and become consistent for a while, they are not accurate.

To understand this better, consider the two fundamental characteristics of optimum orientation: *consistent perception* and *accurate perception*. If we have consistent perception, even if it is inaccurate, we can learn how to read, write, spell and do maths. Most non-dyslexic people have consistent perception because of their stable orientation, whereas dyslexics do not.

For all the senses except balance and motion, some degree of inaccuracy will not greatly affect the person's ability to read, listen, speak or write. A person who is tone-deaf won't be able to sing well, but can carry on a conversation with no trouble. A person who is colour-blind won't be able to paint a realistic picture, but can easily read a newspaper article.

However, distortions in the senses of balance and motion will always cause some degree of clumsiness. The primary sources of our senses of balance and motion are the *vestibular* organs in our inner ear. These organs have tiny 'motion sensor' hairs in liquid-filled chambers that work on a principle similar to a carpenter's spirit level. Imagine hanging pictures on a wall with a level that is not properly aligned. You will end up with a wall full of consistently crooked pictures.

The senses of balance and motion are regulated by

gravity and the environment. For uncorrected dyslexics with dyspraxia, even when they are not disorientated, the orientation they experience is not providing them with accurate vestibular perception. Any distortion—even if it is consistent—will give the person an incorrect view of the physical environment, and will become obvious in the person's physical responses.

Dyspraxia makes sense, because if the senses of balance and movement are either temporarily distorted or inherently inaccurate, we would expect to see clumsy or awkward behaviour.

All dyslexics will, from time to time, experience some degree of dyspraxia because of disorientations. It shows up as a chronic condition in only about ten to fifteen per cent of dyslexic children. Like the other aspects of dyslexia, it varies in severity.

The chronic clumsiness caused by inaccurate perception is solved when the Fine Tuning procedures described in Chapters 29 and 30 are done. The sporadic clumsiness caused by disorientation will gradually be resolved as the dyslexia itself is solved by gaining mastery of the symbols of language.

CHAPTER 12

A Real Solution

What every dyslexic needs is the ability to think with the symbols and words that trigger disorientation. These words are already part of the dyslexic's speaking vocabulary, but the dyslexic probably couldn't give a definition if asked for one, and doesn't have a mental picture of the word's meaning.

Until the person fully understands the trigger words and can use them in his or her thought process, any remedial work may make the problem worse, not better.

This seems to be a sticky situation. Dyslexic people need to learn to think with the very words that cause disorientation. Being exposed to these words will cause them to distort the data they are trying to learn. If we provide a definition for the word, we have already defeated the purpose, because everything dyslexics hear or read in a disorientated state is altered and incorrect. It is like asking them to walk into a fire without being burned.

The impasse is like a closed circuit or a 'Catch-22'. The action that should solve the problem is creating the problem.

ORIENTATION COUNSELLING

The way to move beyond this impasse is by giving the dyslexic a method to control the disorientations that occur when trigger words are encountered. A simple procedure called Davis Orientation Counselling teaches the dyslexic a technique for terminating or turning off disorientations. Once the person learns how to eliminate the multiple perceptions, he can experience a consistent, undistorted viewpoint whenever he wishes. Once the technique is learned, it is simple to do anywhere, and takes less than a second. This counselling procedure is covered in Chapter 27.

The result of *orientation* is an accurate, consistent perception of the environment, including two-dimensional words printed on a page. When the dyslexic is orientated, the words on the page are perceived correctly, without distortion. Data can be received accurately.

If a dyslexic can recognise disorientation and consciously produce a state of orientation at will, disorientation can be turned off whenever it occurs. Then the person can acquire the information he needs to learn. Even if disorientating stimuli are encountered and disorientation occurs, it can be corrected quickly. So it no longer prevents accurate perception and learning.

The symptoms of dyslexia are manifestations of disorientation, so terminating the disorientation also terminates the symptoms. The reading skill of most dyslexics improves dramatically as soon as they begin to use this simple process. They may still have problems with words they don't know, but they are at least able to recognise the words they have already learned.

It may seem that the problem is solved simply by controlling the disorientations, but nothing has been done about the real problem at all. In fact, a new problem has been added: constantly checking one's state of orientation and making corrections to stop disorientation.

SYMBOL MASTERY

Dyslexics need to learn to think non-verbally with trigger words. Once they do, there is no need consciously to control disorientations. It was the inability to think with the trigger words that caused the disorientations to occur in the first place. The ability to think with the trigger words will eliminate the disorientations.

This presents a new set of problems for teachers. The traditional teaching methods used in the educational system—at least in the western world—are not well suited to the thought process of a non-verbal thinker. Just having a dyslexic read the definitions of trigger words like *a, and* and *the* from the dictionary, even while maintaining orientation, will not allow the person to *think* with the words. The definitions are only being recited like the Alphabet Song. The meanings of the words are not fully comprehended.

Dyslexics need to form mental pictures they can use to think with, and to associate these pictures visually and auditorily with the words they are trying to learn.

Showing a dyslexic a picture to describe the meaning of a word would seem to be a step in the right direction, but even that doesn't work very well. It requires a tremendous amount of repetition. You might have to flash a picture in front of a dyslexic a thousand times before the person could incorporate that picture into his or her thinking process. Dyslexics usually find rote repetition excruciatingly boring, so they are likely to disorientate into their own thoughts and daydream rather than pay attention to this type of exercise.

Again, there seems to be an impasse. Traditional teaching methods can't get the job done; they only frustrate the student.

CREATING THE CONCEPT

For non-verbal thinkers, an important element has been left out of the education process: creativity. The creative process and the learning process, if not identical, are so closely related that they are inseparable. If there is one thing dyslexics love to do, it is to exercise their creativity.

It's only my opinion, but I think learning should be fun. People seem to learn more easily, thoroughly and quickly when the subject is interesting and entertaining. As human beings, we enjoy pleasurable experiences and seem to have a natural capacity to remember them.

If we want the dyslexic to think with the meaning of a trigger word, the dyslexic should be allowed to *create* a personal mental picture that accurately shows the meaning. Showing him or her a photograph that represents the meaning of a trigger word may be better than saying the definition, but unless the dyslexic actually creates the picture, not much will be gained.

The Davis Symbol Mastery procedure consists of having the person create the meaning of a word or symbol as a three-dimensional picture. The student makes a clay model that illustrates the meaning of the word or symbol, accompanied by a clay figure of the word itself. For abstract words such as articles and prepositions, the clay models take the form of scenarios illustrating the concept or relationship represented. The person then says the word aloud, and makes up sentences using it. By creating the conceptual picture on a table top, with a clay model, and making the sound of the word, the person gains the ability to think with that word or symbol in both verbal and non-verbal modes. The Davis Symbol Mastery procedures are described fully in Chapters 31 and 33.

Once all the trigger words that stimulate disorientation are mastered with Symbol Mastery, the dyslexic will no longer have a learning disability. The root causes of the disability have been eliminated, so compulsive solutions are no longer being triggered. The 'old solution' behaviours will continue for a while, but the dyslexic will gradually experience easier ways of doing things. The old solution will be dropped, and the one that works better will be adopted. The new solution will not be compulsive like the old solution because it is done consciously, with full understanding. At this point, it would be safe to say that the person's dyslexia is corrected.

How I Finally Learned The Alphabet

As a child, I had a problem called autism. It is like super-dyslexia, only with more severe disorientations triggered by auditory stimuli. At the age of twelve, I still hadn't learned the alphabet. Even the Alphabet Song couldn't get me past the letter G.

The alphabet was displayed on a banner across the top of a blackboard at school, but I couldn't keep the letters straight. They always seemed to be turning upside down, reversing into mirror images or appearing in a different place.

One thing I could do was make highly detailed models of things from muddy clay I dug out of a small pit in the back garden. One day, I formed a D, an F and an O from ropes of clay and left them to dry on the ground. The next day, the D, F and O on the banner at school kept still and stayed in their correct places. When I went home to check I discovered that I had made only one mistake: my clay F was backwards. That was easy to fix by flipping it over.

I had memorised the shapes of a few more letters that day, so I proceeded to make them out of clay. I kept adding a couple of letters each day until I had all 26, arranged in the order they appeared on the chart. Once I had done this, I knew the forms of all the capital letters and their correct sequence.

This experience helped me develop the Davis Symbol Mastery procedure.

PART TWO

Little P.D.—
A Developmental
Theory of Dyslexia

'Every time we
teach a child something,
we prevent him from
inventing it himself.'

— Jean Piaget

CHAPTER 13

How Dyslexia Happens

Apparently, some people are born with a genetic code that enables them to utilise the part of their brain that alters and creates perceptions. Being born with this genetic code doesn't give them dyslexia, it only makes it possible for them to develop it. This theory explains why dyslexia seems to run in families and why many experts consider it to be hereditary.

Developing dyslexia involves some rather complex steps, and the timing has to be precise. In fact, developing dyslexia is so complicated that it's a wonder anyone can do it.

AN EARLY START

A dyslexic didn't start to develop dyslexia in his first few years at school, or even at nursery school. It started long before that. The dyslexic began using the special talent that brings about dyslexia possibly as early as the age of three months.

Probably it is between the ages of three and six months that dyslexics begin the development of their special abilities, skills and deficiencies. I have an idea that if an infant starts using the distortion function of the brain before the age of three months, the resulting problems will be far more severe than dyslexia. This might result in such inaccurate perceptions that the person could not relate to the outside world normally. The person would probably be labelled *autistic* or regarded as having a *learning disability*.

THE POTENTIAL DYSLEXIC IN INFANCY

Psychologists say a three-month-old infant is just beginning to recognise facial features. That means the infant can focus the eyes and control convergence of the two mental images they produce; otherwise it couldn't even see a face. Although a three-month-old can see, the child hasn't yet learned to control its neck muscles in order to look in a certain direction. The child simply sees whatever happens to move into its field of vision.

Let's create a scenario of a Potential Dyslexic, P.D. for short. Let's make little P.D. three months old and put him in a cot. From his perspective, all little P.D. can see is the end of a chest of drawers with someone's elbow sticking out past the edge.

If little P.D. happens to trigger the brain cells that alter his perception, he will no longer see what his eyes see, he will see something else. At that point, if P.D. is curious about who the elbow belongs to, it would be very easy for him simply to add the other features to the elbow and see the face of the person.

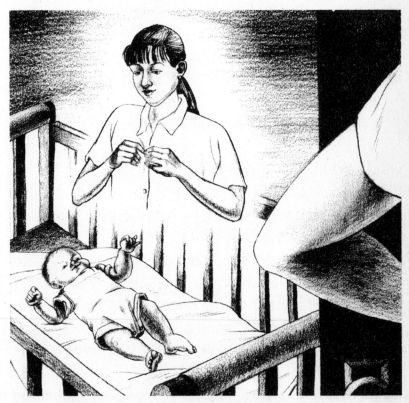

When little P.D. disorientates his perceptions, a glimpse of his mother's elbow provides him with a complete mental image of her. Once he exercises this ability successfully, he continues using it to explore his environment.

When he sees the face, he can recognise whether or not it's the person who feeds him.

We don't fully understand what little P.D. has just done. It seems to border on the supernatural, but that is only because we don't fully understand the nature of intuitive thought. Perhaps it was a subliminal mental association between the arm P.D. has just seen and his mental image of the face he has already seen.

Through whatever means, little P.D. actually saw a face in his mind as real as the one he would see with his eyes, and recognised it as the face of his mother.

This mental talent P.D. uses to recognise an object never seems to make a mistake. His 'self-created' perceptions always seem to be accurate as to what or who the object is.

Of course, there's another way to recognise another person by seeing only an elbow: through analytical reasoning and logic. P.D. doesn't have those conscious skills yet. Children don't begin to develop them until about the age of three years. P.D. didn't think about anything or go through the process of elimination, he just *used* disorientation.

So here is little three-month-old P.D. recognising things in his environment that he shouldn't be able to recognise for three more years. This ability he has for recognising real objects in his environment will influence the rest of his early childhood development.

Little P.D.'s other early childhood skills may develop more rapidly than normal, or they may be delayed. He will probably have some areas of accelerated development and some of delayed development, both stemming from the same cause: his ability mentally to complete fragmentary perceptions.

The Visual Buffer

Dr Stephen Kosslyn, a Harvard University psychologist, says the visual centre of the brain contains a 'visual buffer' where images are perceived and sent to the upper conceptual centres of the brain for processing. The converse also occurs when thoughts and stored visual images are sent back to the visual buffer. There they are perceived as visual images for purposes of recognition by what he also calls 'the mind's eye'.

The real and mental images can be combined and confused, he says. An example is the fact that eyewitnesses of crimes or accidents often believe they saw what their expectations told them to see—not what actually happened.

Kosslyn, S. M. (1994). *Image and brain: The resolution of the imagery debate*. Cambridge, MA; MIT Press.

CHAPTER 14

The Two-Year-Old and the Kitten

Let's look at the next stage of little P.D.'s development, beginning around the age of two years. He is becoming very curious. Too curious, his parents say. He is getting into everything. Little P.D. has explored every inch of his environment including under the sink, inside cupboards, inside the laundry basket, and everywhere else that it was possible for him to get into. He has dumped everything out of every box and bottle he could get his hands on and probably tasted most of it. He is so environmentally aware that his parents can't bring something new into the house without his finding it almost immediately.

Let's see how well little P.D.'s dyslexic talents are progressing by giving him a little white kitten. But instead of handing it to him, let's curl it up into a tight white ball and put it in the corner of the living room. Then let's have little P.D. toddle into the room. He doesn't get more than three steps into the room before his attention is drawn to the ball of fur in the corner. As soon as his eyes track to it, he begins to totter, rocking back and forth. In less than a second he exclaims, 'Kitty!' and heads for the ball of fluff in the corner.

How could a two-year-old child recognise a white ball of fur as a kitten, not as a bunny or some furry toy? The same way he could recognise his mother almost two years earlier. As soon as his eyes tracked to the object and he didn't recognise what it was, he experienced a feeling of confusion. The feeling of confusion triggered the part of the brain that alters his perception. He momentarily lost his sense of balance. The room became silent. His inner clock skipped a beat. During that instant, his perceptual talent allowed him to look at the ball of fur from every angle and direction.

But the kitten was rolled up tightly. A ball of fur is only a ball of fur from every view. So how could he recognise it?

If little P.D. has ever seen something come apart, like groceries out of a grocery bag or a gift being unwrapped, that process has already been incorporated into his thinking process. So after he used his perceptual ability to look at the ball of fur from every possible direction, it began to come apart in his mental image. Out came a paw, then another paw and a tail, then out popped the head and P.D. recognised the kitten.

As soon as the recognition occurred, P.D.'s feeling of confusion disappeared. The disorientation function of his brain shut off. At that moment P.D. regained his sense of balance, so he didn't fall down, he only tottered. At the same moment his hearing turned on again, his internal clock started ticking again, and he dived for the kitten in the corner.

P.D. isn't aware that his brain has just looked at possibly 2,000 views of what that ball of fur might be. It happened too fast. The most little P.D. could be aware of would be a blurring of his vision for two blinks of his eyes, a sensation of floating, or a feeling of sinking. He may even have felt a little queasy. But the entire episode was over so fast that he hardly noticed.

By the age of two, little P.D. is automatically and unconsciously using the function of disorientation to recognise objects in his environment. He is rewarded for using it, because the process never seems to make a mistake.

CHAPTER 15

Ages Three to Five

What happens between the ages of three and five will make it possible for little P.D. to be more intelligent than normal, but will also create the potential for him to develop a learning disability.

In normal childhood development, the skills for analytical reasoning and logic should begin to develop at around the age of three. These are the skills for *consciously* recognising people by seeing elbows, and kittens by seeing white balls of fur. Children who need these skills begin to develop them. But little P.D. already has a system that is faster and more accurate than analytical reasoning and logic ever could be. He has no need of those skills at all, so they don't develop.

Children who need skills of analytical reasoning and logic must also start to develop their skills of verbal conceptualisation, because reasoning and logic are language-based processes. These forms of thinking occur in the same patterns as sentences. So a normal child must use the speech and language centre on the left side of the brain in his or her thought process.

This explains why verbal conceptualisation is many times slower than non-verbal conceptualisation: The speech and language centre of the brain must, of necessity, operate at the maximum intelligible speed of speech—at most, perhaps 250 words per minute, or about four words per second. The result is that the normal child's thinking process is dramatically slowing down, while P.D.'s mind continues to race along at full speed.

P.D. has, of course, learned to understand spoken language, and can talk. In fact, he sometimes tries to talk as fast as he can think, and his mouth can't keep up with his mind. When he is trying to say something he considers important, his speech speeds up so much that the words run together. What his parents hear is an unintelligible garble of sounds. They worry that he is developing a stutter.

'Slow down, darling,' says his mother. 'You're talking so fast I can't understand what you're saying.' To P.D., who is trying to describe a thought he is visualising, her speech sounds agonisingly slow.

It's as if she is speaking at the rate of less than one . . . word . . . per . . . second.

Estimates of the speed differential between verbal and non-verbal conceptualisation range from 400 to 2,000 times faster when people use the non-verbal mode. The reality is probably somewhere in between.

The process of developing verbal conceptualisation skills (thinking with the sound of language) can take up to two years. Once it fully develops, it will become the primary thinking mode of most children. So by the age of five, at about the time primary school begins, the normal children have already begun to think with the sounds of words. This may be slow, but it will come in handy when they begin learning how to read.

Meanwhile, although he has heard people say things and has said quite a lot himself, P.D. hasn't ever *heard* one of his own thoughts. He has been too busy thinking with pictures—a thought process that happens so fast, he doesn't even notice he's doing it.

CHAPTER 16

The First Day of School

To see the effect of non-verbal thinking on little P.D., let's make him five years old and send him to primary school. No matter how prepared he was for this day, and no matter how enthusiastically he was looking forward to it, the reality is terrifying.

He is in a strange place. There he sits. He's scared to death. He would rather be anywhere else in the world than where he is.

Now let's have a strange lady go up to the blackboard with a piece of chalk and write the letters *C-A-T*. She turns round and says, 'Who knows what this is?' Some of the other kids have already learned the word, but P.D. doesn't know. Even when they say 'cat', he makes no connection. The lines don't form anything like his mental picture of a cat.

When he looked at the lines on the board and didn't recognise what they were, he experienced the feeling of confusion. By this time, confusion *automatically* triggers the area of his brain that alters his perception. Within a blink of his eyes, his brain looks at the word in at least forty different configurations. He perceives the word forwards, backwards, upside-down both ways, and floating in space from various perspectives.

Then, in another blink, because it still has not been recognised, the word will be pulled apart and reassembled in every possible configuration just like the image of the white, furry cat when he was two. Only this time it won't work.

P.D. isn't aware that his brain has just taken in all those conflicting pieces of data. The most he could have noticed is that things may have gone blurry for two blinks of his eyes. He may have had the sensation of floating or sinking, and he may have felt a little sick. But most of all he felt confused.

STUMPED

For the first time in his life, P.D.'s special method for recognising things didn't work. It not only failed to recognise the word and get rid of the confusion, it made the word at least forty times more confusing. He was trying to understand the word not as a symbol, but as an object.

Had the teacher shown him a real cat, P.D. would have recognised it within two blinks of his eyes, even if it were rolled up into a tight ball of fur. He could

CATTACIAƆCɅ⊥
ƆATTACIAƆƆɅ⊥
CAⅡACⅡAƆƆɅ⊥
ACTTƆAIƆɅɅC⅃
ɅCTTƆɅACⅡ⅃A
AƆTTCAɅƆⅡCA
ATCƆTAɅ⅃CƆIɅ
CTAATƆCIɅɅ⅃Ɔ
A⅃CƆ⅃AɅTCƆTɅ
ɅTƆCTɅA⅃ƆCIA

Forty dyslexic variations of the word CAT.

have done that three years before he entered the classroom. But the teacher didn't show him a cat; she showed him the word *CAT*. The same function his brain would perform to recognise the object almost instantly produced multiple dyslexic distortions of the word with no resolution of his confusion.

If we look at this from a different perspective, P.D. has just put at least 40 pieces of data into his mental computer. Thirty-nine pieces of data were incorrect.

The only method little P.D. has for determining the correct data is the process of elimination. So, without anyone showing him or telling him how to do it, he eventually happens upon it by himself.

Some time after he begins doing the process of elimination, the teacher will come past and say something like 'P.D., dear, you're not supposed to guess. Here, try . . .' What he was doing looked exactly like guessing, but it wasn't.

By the time little P.D. has done all the things he must do to recognise the word *CAT*, he will have performed at least four thousand times more computations in his brain than the other children. It's true that he can think between four hundred and two thousand times faster than most other children. But because he has to do at least four thousand times more, he will appear very *slow*.

INVALIDATION

The teacher's remark may seem trivial, but it is essential to the creation of dyslexia. Until someone tells P.D. that his method of dealing with incorrect data and confusion is wrong, he won't manifest the emotional reactions associated with the learning disability of dyslexia.

If the invalidation happens in his first year at school, he will develop dyslexia then. If it doesn't happen until his fourth year, he won't have dyslexia until his fourth year. The struggle to comprehend will be there, but he won't become aware that he is different from other children, and won't lose his sense of self-esteem.

Even little P.D. isn't aware that he is using the process of elimination. He isn't aware that he has at least 39 pieces of incorrect data for every three-letter word he has failed to recognise.

He isn't aware that the process he is using to eliminate incorrect data is the only one available to him if he wants to arrive at a correct answer. At his age, he doesn't know the difference between guessing and making mistakes. As far as he is concerned, he is making mistakes.

No one likes making mistakes, so little P.D. has the natural human reaction to mistakes. He gets upset. Before long, his emotional reactions upset the teacher. The teacher in turn upsets the school administration, and they upset P.D.'s parents.

Someone will eventually tell the parents that P.D. is immature or a slow developer, or some such thing. They usually don't use the words *subnormal* or *stupid*, but the message comes across clearly.

Once P.D. gets upset about making his mistakes, everyone is bound to get upset with him, so he becomes increasingly frustrated. He is frustrated because these word things should be easy, as easy as everything else. But they aren't; they're impossible.

At this point, P.D. has acquired the emotional distress he needs to become a fully fledged dyslexic.

CHAPTER 17

The Age of Disability

At about the age of nine, when he is in his fifth year at school, young P.D. reaches his limit of frustration. If he doesn't discover a way to get over, under, round, or through his problem with words, he'll be stuck in that form for the rest of his life. By now school has become torture, so he's desperate.

P.D. begins to solve his problem. He finds mental tricks and gimmicks like rote memorisation and associations of sounds, songs, rhymes—and worst of all, concentration. These allow him to function in the world of words. Everyone is happy for him now that he is at last making some progress. He has finally started to learn his lessons, but the lessons have little to do with genuine learning. The lessons he learns will comprise a lifelong disability. They are compulsive behaviours. At best, they may enable him to get by in school as a 'slow' student who 'tries hard'.

P.D. has begun the process of accumulating his 'old solutions'. He is beginning to change a limitation into a disability. It was a limitation because he had to perform thousands of times more computations than the other students just to recognise three-letter words. It will become a disability because he has no control over his 'old solutions'. They control him.

If P.D. finds himself in a remedial education class, he will have the opportunity to acquire more of these ruses than if he stayed in an ordinary class. Remedial teachers are usually very good at passing their own 'old solutions' along to their students. This can make it appear that children are making at least a little progress. Unfortunately, being in a remedial class also lowers P.D.'s self-esteem even more. It convinces him beyond a doubt that he is lacking in intelligence. In his first year, they only hinted about his stupidity. Now it has been confirmed.

If he isn't put into a remedial class, P.D. may be held back a year or even two years during primary school. Being a year or two older than the other children may be embarrassing in the classroom, but his size and advanced development in non-academic areas may provide him with advantages in physical education, music and art, as well as during break and in after-school activities.

To compensate and find some form of self-esteem, P.D. may adopt any number of interests, none of which has to do with reading and writing. It could be a sport, visual arts, music or acting. It could be rebellion. If he decides to be naughty as a defence, and gives his parents and teachers trouble, he may discover he has a real talent for delinquency.

During his teenage years, his talent for sizing up a situation and motivating others may provide opportunities for leadership, whether in a school club, sports, a part-time job or a gang.

It would be easy to blame the problem of dyslexia on the educational system, but according to the basic premise of dyslexia presented here, it's clear that the dyslexic created the condition. P.D. is responsible for all the actions that produced the learning disability. He alone learned to distort his perceptions. If we try to put that responsibility anywhere else, his problems will never be completely resolved. Of course he was unaware of his actions, but that doesn't alter the fact that only P.D. can learn to undo what he has done.

THE DYSLEXIC GROWS UP

To P.D., school classes that involve reading and writing are mental torture chambers. He learns much of what is taught in art, music and science, because the teachers in those classes rely on verbal instruction and demonstration. But his written test scores are low, even in the courses he enjoys. Since everyone says education is important, P.D. completes as much school as he can tolerate. He may leave at the age of sixteen and get a job that allows him to use his excellent mechanical abilities. He may stay on after GCSEs and excel at sports, art or acting. If he's lucky, he may find a girlfriend to help him with English papers.

Later, he may struggle through college and go into business, even though his reading level forces him to operate on a semi-illiterate basis wherever written communications are concerned.

STILL USING THE TALENTS

Whatever else P.D. does, he does not lose the initial gift he developed of looking at an object or situation and 'just knowing' what it is. As he continues to observe the world, he also develops a keen, intuitive understanding of how things work. He is imaginative and inventive. He is visually and kinaesthetically orientated. He is able to think on his feet and react quickly. He is a good athlete, conversationalist, salesman or storyteller. If his self-esteem drops to a low enough level, he may become socially inept. Even so, he will find some way to maintain at least a little self-esteem, even if it is at the emotional expense of others.

Still, he does have a low opinion of himself, because he has spent at least half his life hearing people describe him explicitly or implicitly as stupid or handicapped. He secretly hides his inability to read well, and invents ever more tricks and gimmicks to beat the system of the written word.

Along the way, he may take seminars and self-improvement courses that attempt to 'cure' or help him cope with his disability. Some might help. Some might introduce more compulsive solutions in the form of conditioned behaviours. Some might help him learn things that have nothing to do with reading or writing. Most likely, he will simply find ways to do what he can do well and avoid what he can't do. If he has a job that requires him to fill out reports, he will find a way to get someone else to do them.

Some day, he might discover that he is talented at a visual art like sculpting. In fact, because he can visualise the form he wants to sculpt, he can do it effortlessly. To make a bust, all he has to do is place an image of someone's head inside a block of wood or clay and carve the excess material from around the edges. Or he can put an image of the head on a table and fill it with material as if it were an invisible mould.

This last specific example is from my own life. In fact, many of little P.D.'s experiences were really those of little R.D.—Ron Davis.

A Discovery

In 1980, I was lucky enough to discover how to correct the severe perceptual distortions that had been my everyday reality for 38 years.

I was working as a sculptor when another artist wrote and asked me about my sculpting technique. His letter was so filled with praise that I began the laborious process of composing a response. Hours later, after carefully getting my thoughts down, I discovered that the letter was totally illegible—just a bunch of meaningless scrawls that nobody could ever read.

Months later, it occurred to me that when I wrote the letter, I had been focusing on my creative process. I wondered if this was what had made my dyslexia worse. The engineer in me reasoned that if my dyslexia could be changed by something I was doing mentally, it could not possibly be a structural problem but must be a functional problem. Thus, there had to be something I could do mentally to correct my dyslexia. This was my first step as a researcher in the field of learning disabilities.

Three days later, I managed to work out how to correct my perceptual distortions. I went to the library, picked up Treasure Island *and, for the first time in my life, read a book from cover to cover in just a few hours.*

Since then, I have worked at developing techniques based on what I discovered. I have had the pleasure of helping more than 1,000 dyslexic children and adults learn to make the words—and the world—stand still.

PART THREE

The Gift

The Gifted Vintner

Mark was eight when he came to the Reading Research Council. He had struggled through three years of school, but was performing below the level of a six-year-old. His teachers had suggested that he be tested for neurological damage. This didn't make sense to his mother. Even though he was doing poorly at school, she knew he had special gifts in many areas.

Mark's family were fourth-generation vintners. Since he was four, his grandfather had been taking him along to the vineyards and the winery. To Mark, the art and science of wine making were play. By the age of six, he could tell when the time was right to pick and press the grapes. He just knew when the sugar content was right, or when the acid in the skins wasn't. He could tell when fermentation was complete, when to move the wines from vats to barrels, and from barrels to bottles. If you asked him how he knew, he would just tap the side of his head with his finger. His great-grandfather had had the same sense for the grapes, considered the greatest gift a vintner can possess.

When Mark's mother read a story in the local newspaper about our work, the list of dyslexia symptoms I had given to the reporter caught her eye. One was intuitive thinking ability, whereby some dyslexics just know things without any understanding of how or why.

She explained, 'The symptoms in the article matched so many things I'd noticed about Mark when he was little. He rarely cried. He walked before he crawled. He started talking much earlier than all my friends' babies. He could remember events perfectly, even those that happened when he was an infant. Yet he could hardly say the alphabet or spell his own name. I had never heard dyslexia described that way before, but it fitted my son like a glove. Until then I had no idea that Mark's special abilities and his learning problems were related.'

CHAPTER 18

Understanding the Talent

Like the negative side of dyslexia, where no two people have the same disabilities, the gift of dyslexia is different for each person. There are, however, general characteristics that all dyslexics have in common.

Like its negative aspect, the gift of dyslexia is developmental. It has to grow. It must be created by the dyslexic. Over a period of time it changes. Often it doesn't fully develop until the dyslexic has been out of school for a number of years. Perhaps the intervening years are a sort of recovery period.

The eventual gift of dyslexia will be the gift of *mastery*. The dyslexic will be able to master many skills faster than the average person could comprehend or understand them.

The gift of mastery is an accumulation of various characteristics of the individual's basic abilities. It begins with the characteristic of non-verbal thought.

PICTURE THINKING

The primary thought process of the dyslexic is a non-verbal picture thinking mode which occurs at 32 pictures per second. In a second, a verbal thinker could have between two and five thoughts (individual words conceptualised) while a picture thinker would have thirty-two (individual pictures conceptualised). Mathematically, this works out at between six and ten times as many thoughts.

There is also the principle expressed by the old adage '*A picture is worth a thousand words*'. A picture thinker could think a single picture of a concept that might require hundreds or thousands of words to describe. Einstein's theory of relativity came to him in a *daydream* in which he travelled beside a beam of light. His vision lasted only seconds, yet spawned scores of textbooks that attempt to explain it. To Einstein, the concept was simple; to the average person, it is nearly incomprehensible.

Picture thinking is estimated to be, overall, 400 to 2,000 times faster than verbal thinking. Obviously, it varies with the complexity of the individual pictures. But there is more to it than just a difference in speed. Picture thinking is more thorough, deeper, and more comprehensive.

Verbal thought is linear in time, performed by making sentences one word at a time, whereas picture thinking is evolutionary. The picture grows as the mental process adds more sub-concepts to the overall concept.

Pictured thoughts are as thorough or deep as these mental pictures are accurate in portraying the meanings of the words that the person would use to describe the same thoughts.

We could say pictured thoughts are of *substance* while verbal thoughts are *significant sound*.

INTUITION

The only drawback to picture thinking is that the person doing it is not aware of the individual pictures as they occur. It happens too fast. The *incidence of awareness* is the amount of time it takes for something to register consciously in the awareness of the individual. In humans it is fairly consistent at 1/25 of a second. In other words, a stimulus must be present for 1/25 of a second in order to register in the person's consciousness.

If a stimulus is present longer than 1/25 second, we are aware of it. This is called *cognizance*. If a stimulus is present for less than 1/25 of a second, but longer than 1/36 of a second, it falls into the category called *subliminal*. Our brain gets it, but we aren't aware of what it got. If it is part of a continuum, it fuses with the pictures that precede and follow. If a stimulus isn't present for at least 1/36 of a second, we don't even get it subliminally. It went by too fast for our brain to catch it at all.

Picture thinking seems to be consistently happening at about thirty-two pictures per second, or a frequency of 1/32 of a second, the same speed as the flicker-fusion rate of the eye—in other words, the eye's shutter speed.

This is somewhat faster than the incidence of awareness at 1/25 of a second, but slower than the subliminal limit of 1/36 of a second. So picture thinking falls within the subliminal band.

The person's brain gets the thought, but the person isn't consciously aware of it. As a result, we can begin to understand *intuition*, because picture thinking is the same as intuitive thinking. The person becomes aware of the product of the thought process as soon as it occurs, but is not aware of the process as it is happening. The person knows the answer without knowing why it is the answer.

Many dyslexics find a way to bring the subliminal thought process into their awareness. If they think of something interesting, they can disorientate into the thought and watch the individual pictures as they occur. When they do this, it is called a *daydream*. Parents and teachers are very critical of daydreaming, but they shouldn't be. In fact, they should encourage it at every opportunity. Daydreaming is the process of genius, as Einstein and others have proved time and again.

The Incidence of Awareness

TV frames appear on the screen at a speed of 25 frames per second, fast enough to trick our eyes into seeing smooth motion. Modern films, projected at 24 frames per second, trick our eyes most of the time, but occasionally make the wheels of a stagecoach appear to spin backwards. Old silent films run at 16 frames per second appear noticeably jerky. Our brains can easily catch the jumps between individual pictures.

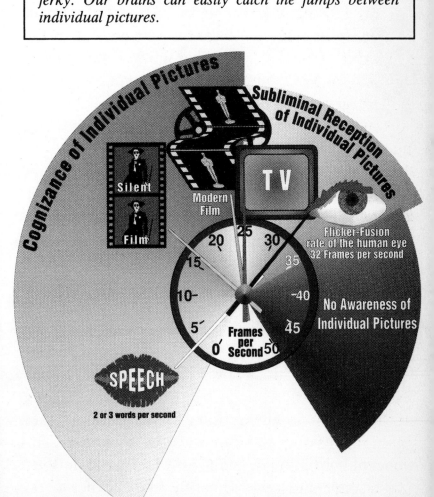

MULTIDIMENSIONAL THOUGHT

Disorientation adds dimension to the thought process. The thinking is no longer subliminal, nor only in pictures. Multidimensional thought uses all the senses.

When a disorientation has occurred, the brain no longer sees what the eyes are looking at, but what the person is thinking, *as though* the eyes were seeing it. The brain no longer hears what the ears are hearing, but what the person is thinking, *as though* the ears were hearing it. The body no longer feels what its senses are feeling, but what the person is thinking, and so on.

One aspect of multidimensional thinking is the ability of the thinker to experience thoughts as realities.

Reality is what the person perceives it to be, and the disorientation alters the perception. The person's thoughts become the person's perceptions, so the thoughts are *reality* to that individual.

A CREATIVE PROCESS

If 'necessity is the mother of invention', then multidimensional thinking must be its father. This concept helps us understand how Leonardo da Vinci could conceptualise a submarine 300 years before the invention of a device that could pump the water out of it. We see how he could imagine a helicopter 400 years before there was an engine that could power one. There is little doubt that Leonardo experienced flight and underwater travel hundreds of years before they became realities. His multidimensional ability allowed him to experience his thoughts as realities and draw the results for everyone else to see.

Of course, there were probably people in Leonardo's day who considered these ideas crazy.

On the darker side, we can also begin to understand why mental institutions have numerous residents who are absolutely convinced they are Jesus Christ or Napoleon. Their problem is they cannot distinguish between imaginary reality and the reality shared by most people.

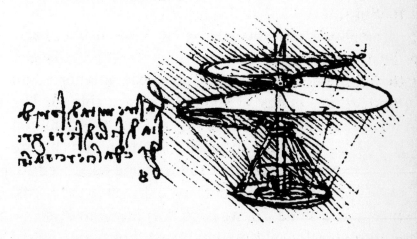

Leonardo visualised human-powered flight in this helicopter sketch. It is described by a note in the 'mirror image' handwriting he used in his notebooks.

CHAPTER 19

Curiosity

From as early as the age of three months, a dyslexic has used disorientation to recognise objects in the environment. This ability is extremely accurate, seeming never to err. By the time a dyslexic is two years old, the disorientations have become automatic, occurring whenever the person encounters confusion.

The ability to recognise objects at such an early age makes dyslexics highly aware of the environment. As a result, dyslexic infants begin 'getting into things' as soon as they are able to. The drive to become mobile is very strong. It is common for dyslexic children to begin walking months before child development books say they are supposed to.

It is common for parents to be driven to their wits' end trying to devise ways of keeping their dyslexic children *in* the places they want them, and *out* of places where they don't want them.

The Crawling Treatment

One of the stranger treatments for dyslexia, from the 1950s, sprang from the observation that children who later developed dyslexia had often begun to walk before they could crawl. The treatment was to make the dyslexics crawl around on the floor until the dyslexia went away. Of course it didn't work, but crawling therapy was added to many treatment programmes for dyslexia, and is still practised in some today.

We can understand the reaction of a mother who has just discovered her two-year-old child under the kitchen sink emptying the contents of all the boxes and bottles. This is dangerous behaviour. Who knows what the child might have eaten? Even after a cooler head has prevailed, it is a behaviour that must be changed.

We can't expect a child of this age to respond to rational arguments. Disciplining the child isn't the answer either, because the child is responding to an urge stronger than normal and one that usual disciplinary procedures will not correct. Besides, if we really understood what the child was doing, we wouldn't want to change it. So child-proofing the kitchen and bathroom cupboards and putting plastic covers over doorknobs would be a better solution than punishment.

The dyslexic child isn't getting into things just to upset the parents. The child is responding to an urge that will eventually become part of the gift of dyslexia.

The seed that has begun to grow is *curiosity*. Curiosity is a stronger force than gravity. If it weren't, there would be no aeroplanes. Curiosity is more important than knowledge: it is the root of knowledge. Without it there would be no such thing as knowledge.

Most importantly, curiosity is the dynamic force behind creativity. Without creativity, mankind would still be living in caves.

CHAPTER 20

Creativity

Creativity is what sets mankind above other life forms. It is believed that God, the creator, made man in His image. If this is so, man in the image of God must be creative.

In the dyslexic, the creative urge is profoundly stronger than in individuals who do not possess the dyslexic's basic abilities. Because of *picture thinking*, *intuitive thought*, *multidimensional thought* and *curiosity*, the dyslexic's creativity is greatly enhanced.

Creativity allows us to conceive of things which don't actually exist. From that experience, we can bring new things into existence. All original ideas stem from the creative process.

We think of creativity as invention or innovation. That is correct, but on a more basic level, creativity is the means by which real learning takes place.

Conditioning is a very rudimentary form of learning. When we train a dog to do tricks, we condition the animal through rewards or penalties to behave in a desired manner. Humans can also be conditioned in this way, but it is much more difficult. Often the conditioning isn't effective.

Because of creativity, humans learn on a much higher level. The act of reasoning is a function of creativity. Logic is a product of creativity. Reasoning and logic are the foundations of learning. If we touch something that burns our fingers, it is with reasoning and logic that we work out why we shouldn't touch it again. We *learned* not to touch it.

In Chapter 15, I mentioned that dyslexic children often haven't developed their skills in reasoning and logic by the time they start school. What they have developed is a variation of these skills that does not follow the linear model of verbal thought. Their analytical reasoning and logic are comparative, using pictures instead of words. This method might be great for working out the helical structure of DNA, but could be useless in attempting to do a maths story problem at school.

Sometimes, like autistic savants, dyslexics can 'see' the answers to maths problems without using pen and paper. This is actually a highly developed form of reasoning. They solved the problem whether or not they bothered to go through the conventional steps. Often, investigation reveals that they have developed highly creative mathematical short cuts.

If the creative process and the human learning

process are not exactly the same process, they are so closely related that they cannot be separated.

Assuming a dyslexic is inherently more creative than the average person, the dyslexic should also be able to *learn* more in less time. Theoretically this is true, but things may appear otherwise to teachers and parents.

The probable reason is that so much education is done on the *conditioning* level. The child is told to go through a series of rote steps without seeing any personal benefit in arriving at a solution.

Dyslexia shouldn't be called a learning disability. It should more accurately be called a *conditioning liability*.

In real life situations, such as on-the-job training, athletics and the arts, dyslexics do learn more in less time than the average person. In fact, when learning is presented experientially, dyslexics can master many things faster than the average person can comprehend them.

Spots in the Air

Until the age of 13, I was disorientated so much of the time that I was thought to have a profound learning disability. Today, I would be classified as autistic. Consequently, I have very few 'real' memories of my childhood. But I'm sure that the following incident, related to me by my mother, is true.

When I was nine years old, my maths teacher was puzzled by the fact that, while I couldn't work out simple problems, I could instantly come up with the answer to complex algebraic equations. One day he discussed this with my mother and asked me, 'If X is one and Y is seven, what is two Y minus X?'

I instantly answered, 'Thirteen'. When asked how I got the answer, I said I saw it. When asked what it looked like, I touched two spots in the air, then touched three more spots under those.

The maths teacher mentioned that he had heard of people called 'savants' who could do this sort of thing.

'You mean idiot savants?' asked my mother indignantly. She castigated the teacher for calling me an idiot, grabbed me by the arm and marched me out of school. After that, I was taken out of the class and not allowed to take any more maths until I was at secondary school, when I took algebra.

In algebra, I correctly answered every problem in the book, every problem the teacher put on the blackboard, and every problem in the tests. Yet I was bottom of the class. The teacher explained that the purpose of the class wasn't just to get right answers; it was to learn how to do the problems. I hadn't done a single one of them. All I had done was write down the answers.

CHAPTER 21

The Gift of Mastery

The gift of dyslexia is the gift of mastery.

When people have mastered something, they have learned it so well they can do it without thinking about what they are doing. Mastering something is *really* learning it. If the creative process and the learning process are the same, then when someone has mastered something, that person has *created* the knowledge it takes to do it.

All real knoweldge is experiential. It is a mistake to confuse the memorisation of data with the understanding of data. And it is a bigger mistake to confuse the understanding of data with knowledge.

When someone has an experience, that person has the knowledge of that experience. If the person then wishes to write that knowledge in a book, the knowledge must be converted into data. When someone else reads the book, the reader doesn't gain the knowledge, but only the data. If the reader understands the data, he or she will only understand the experience conceptually. If the reader *really* wants the knowledge, it will be necessary to have an actual experience similar to that of the author.

If a person wanted to learn how to ride a bicycle, that person could get some books on riding bicycles. After studying all the data in the books, the person might *understand* the principles of riding a bicycle. If the person mistakenly thinks he or she knows how to ride a bicycle, and tries, the experience will quickly demonstrate the difference between *understanding* and *knowing* how to ride the bicycle.

The experience of being on the bicycle gives the rider the opportunity to *create* the act of riding a bicycle. As the person creates riding a bicycle, the person is learning how to ride a bicycle. At first there will be a lot of experimenting, thinking and remembering. As the actual experiences are created, less conscious effort will be needed. When the person can ride automatically without any experimenting, thinking and remembering, the person has mastered riding the bicycle.

This is easy to comprehend for physical skills like riding a bicycle or driving a car, but not so apparent when it comes to learning a language, reading or maths. However, the principle is the same.

When the same principle is applied to learning language skills and maths, dyslexics not only learn these skills, they master them. Davis Symbol Mastery is a process dyslexics can use to apply this principle to anything they want to learn.

Mastery is more than just fast learning. Mastery is a level of learning where conscious thought is no longer required. It is the ability to own the data learned as actual experience. When something is mastered, there is no need to worry about being able to remember it—it's probably impossible to forget.

When someone masters something, it becomes a part of that person. It becomes part of the individual's thought and creative process. It adds the quality of its essence to all subsequent thought and creativity of the individual.

PART FOUR

Doing Something About it

A Guide for Parents and Teachers

Orientation corrects perception.
Symbol Mastery corrects dyslexia.

CHAPTER 22

How Can You Tell?

If you suspect that you or someone you love has the gift of dyslexia, how can it be diagnosed? This seems like a simple, logical question that should have an equally simple, logical answer, but it isn't. If you consider for a moment what you've already read about dyslexia, the reasons for the difficulty will be apparent.

DIVERSE SYMPTOMS, NO PATHOLOGY

The traditional method of diagnosing a problem is to test the person and then study the results with either symptomatology or pathology.

In using symptomatology, the study of symptoms, there are many problems. The first is that no two people who have dyslexia ever exhibit the same symptoms. Until all the people who have dyslexia add their symptoms to the list, we won't even know what all the symptoms might be. In addition, all the known symptoms of dyslexia can result from other causes, including physical disorders such as vision and inner ear problems.

In pathology, the study of the nature of disease, the structural and functional changes in the body caused by disease are studied. The big drawback here is that dyslexia isn't a disease, but a self-created condition.

As the equipment for looking inside bodies becomes more and more sophisticated, there are anomalies we might expect to find, such as a slightly larger pineal gland and more large neurons, which would cause the corpus collosum to be slightly thicker. But considering dyslexia as a developmental process, these anomalies would be a result of the difference in the way the dyslexic's brain develops through use. Saying they cause dyslexia would be incorrect.

These hypothetical differences would also be present in anyone who has the gift of dyslexia, not just those who develop learning disabilities.

As a result, there is no definitive diagnostic test for dyslexia. This is probably the reason why some psychologists and teachers say, 'There is no such thing as dyslexia.' But there is.

If we look at the structure or anatomy of the learning disability known as dyslexia, we find that this developmental sequence occurs:

1 **The individual encounters an unrecognised stimulus.** This could be a word (written or spoken), a symbol, or an object that is not recognised.

2 **The lack of recognition causes a confusion which stimulates disorientation.** The individual uses disorientation mentally to examine the stimulus from different points of view, in an attempt to bring about recognition. This usually works with real-life objects, but doesn't work at all with language, because it is composed of sonic or written symbols for ideas and concepts.

3 **The disorientation causes the assimilation of incorrect data.** The perspectives the individual examines mentally are registered in the brain as actual perceptions. Most of these perceptions are inaccurate.

4 **The assimilation of incorrect data causes the individual to make mistakes.** The individual cannot distinguish between correct and incorrect data, because both are registered in the brain as actual perceptions. The resulting mistakes are usually the first 'symptoms' of dyslexia.

5 **The mistakes cause emotional reactions.** No one likes making mistakes. The individual is simply experiencing a human reaction. This, in turn, causes teachers and parents to react negatively.

6   Emotional reactions bring about frustration. The frustration is a result of the cumulative effects of mistakes and emotional reactions, compounded by the negative responses of other people.

7   Solutions are created or adopted to solve the problems stemming from the use of disorientation in the recognition process. These solutions will be methods of seeming to know things or of performing tasks. Each will have worked at least once and will be a *compulsive behaviour*. The person will use it without even noticing. These 'old solutions' usually begin to accumulate at around the age of nine.

8   The learning disability is composed of the compulsive solutions the individual acquires. Compulsive solutions are mental crutches, rote memorisations, tricks or gimmicks the person uses to give the *appearance* of understanding. They have little if anything to do with actually learning or gaining understanding of the material studied.

9   These compulsive solutions are what disable the learning process. By using compulsive solutions, a person might learn to 'read' the way a parrot learns to talk—without any understanding of the content. Through a few more roundabout mental processes, the person might be able to decipher some of the meaning of the material that is read. But using these solutions is a tedious process.

With this anatomy as a base, we can assess for the characteristics of the mental functions that eventually produce various levels of dyslexia: the ability to do non-verbal conceptualisation and the ability to disorientate the perceptions.

CHAPTER 23

Symptoms of Disorientation

Symptoms are the first things people notice that cause them to suspect a learning disability. We must be familiar with 'known' symptoms, or at least understand the nature of the problem, before we can assess for it.

All of the symptoms of dyslexia are symptoms of disorientation. Dyslexia itself can't be definitively recognised, but disorientation can.

During a disorientation, a person's perceptions become distorted. What is mentally perceived as real is not in agreement with the true facts and conditions in the environment. The main senses that become distorted are vision, hearing, balance, movement and time. Common examples of disorientation include motion sickness, the sense of falling when on an escalator or at the edge of a cliff, 'hearing things' and the false sense of motion people sometimes experience when they are sitting in a stationary vehicle and see another nearby vehicle move.

While a person is disorientated, he or she is not perceiving the same 'reality' as others, and is unaware that what is being perceived is not real.

Thousands of different learning disability symptoms can result from disorientation. The severity and degree to which each of the senses is affected varies from person to person, and from one time to another. The following are just some of the common symptoms of disorientation categorised by the sensory perceptions most affected:

VISION

- Shapes and sequences of letters or numbers appear changed or reversed.

- Spelling is incorrect or inconsistent.

- Words or lines are skipped when reading or writing.

- Letters and numbers appear to move, disappear, grow or shrink.

- Punctuation marks or capital letters are omitted, ignored or not seen.

- Words and letters are omitted, altered or substituted while reading or writing.

HEARING

- Some speech sounds are difficult to make.

- Digraphs such as 'ch' and 'th' are mispronounced.

- 'False' sounds are perceived.

- Appears not to listen or hear what is said.

- Sounds are perceived as quieter, louder, farther away or nearer than actual.

BALANCE/MOVEMENT

- Dizziness or nausea while reading.

- Poor sense of direction.

- Inability to sit still.

- Has difficulty with handwriting.

- Problems with balance and coordination.

TIME

- Hyperactivity (being overactive)

- Hypoactivity (being underactive)

- Maths concepts are difficult to learn

- Difficulty being on time or telling time.

- Excessive daydreaming.

- Train of thought is easily lost.

- Trouble sequencing (putting things in the right order).

COMPULSIVE SOLUTIONS

There are hundreds of compensating behaviours, patterns and mental tricks a person can create or adopt as compulsive solutions to unresolved confusions that slow or stop the ability to learn. Here are some of the more common ones:

- Singing the Alphabet Song.

- Extreme concentration when reading.

- Memorisation.

- Unusual body postures and motions.

- Dependence on others.

- Sounding out every letter of every word.

- Avoidance.

Any combination of the symptoms and behaviours in the five lists above may exist in one individual, while others may be entirely absent.

ABILITY ASSESSMENT

Besides finding symptoms that reveal the negative aspects of disorientation, we can also assess for the presence of four basic abilities shared by dyslexics. These are talents which are part of the gift of dyslexia.

1   The ability intentionally to access the brain's perception distortion function.

2   The ability consciously to view mental images three-dimensionally and move around them in mental space.

3   The ability to experience self-created mental images as real-world phenomena; in other words, experiencing imagination as reality.

4   A tendency or preference to think non-verbally by using pictures of concepts and ideas, with little or no internal monologue.

If these are present, and the individual manifests symptoms of a learning disability, we can safely assume that the symptoms are a result of disorientation and that the person is dyslexic.

Before we get into the step-by-step procedures of assessment and correction, one more concept needs definition. It explains what the person actually does in order to activate the disorientation function of the brain.

CHAPTER 24

The Mind's Eye

What I discovered in December 1980 came as a result of noticing that when I was at 'my artistic best', I was also at 'my dyslexic worst'. Because my symptoms were not constant, this made me question the assumption that dyslexia stemmed from a structural deficit or dysfunction of the brain.

By examining how I viewed things while creating artistically, I discovered that during creative thinking I was shifting the location of the viewpoint that looks at my mental images. I found that by playing with various locations for 'what was doing the looking', I could intentionally increase and decrease the severity of my dyslexia symptoms.

Because I could find no term for 'what was doing the looking', I at first coined the term 'visio-awareness epicentre', or VAE. At the time, this seemed to be a technically correct assemblage of root word concepts, but I preferred something simpler. So I adopted the term 'the mind's eye', which is defined in dictionaries as 'the imagination'.

Later, I discovered that what I termed 'the mind's eye' was also the mental epicentre of other perceptions, such as sound and the sense of balance and motion. So a totally correct term might be 'the mind's epicentre of perception'. I have stuck with 'the mind's eye' because it is an easier concept for people to grasp. This may be because vision is the predominant perception, and the one that usually gives dyslexics the most trouble.

A MENTAL VIEWPOINT

It is important to note that in the Davis procedures, one does not see, look at or sense anything *in*, *through* or *at* the mind's eye. One sees or looks *with*, *from* or *out of* the mind's eye.

Obviously, if you are looking *at* something, you have to be looking *from* somewhere. To put it another way, if you look out of your eyes, you don't see your own face. You can only see a mirror image of it or a photograph of it, but not the face itself, because that is where you are looking from. Similarly, the mind's eye cannot perceive itself. It can only perceive things outside itself, whether they exist in the mind as concepts or in the real world as objects.

When you look at a mental image such as an imagined event or a dream, the mind's eye is what you are looking with, from or out of.

LOCATING THE MIND'S EYE

The mind's eye does have a location. In fact, it has a multitude of possible locations. It is wherever its owner intends it, wishes it or perceives it to be. If this sounds like a supernatural or metaphysical concept, please remember that dyslexics are able to experience their mental images as actual perceptions. So if they place the mind's eye in a particular place, they gain the ability to experience their perceptions from that perspective.

When a dyslexic person looks at an alphabet letter and disorientates, within a split second he or she sees dozens of different views—from the top, the sides and the back of the letter. In other words, the mind's eye is mentally circling round the letter as though it were an object in three-dimensional space. It's like a helicopter buzzing around, doing surveillance on a building. This is the disorientation function hard at work, trying to recognise the object.

Is the mind's eye actually out there in the 'real' world, circling around the letter and moving behind the page of the book? Is the person having an out-of-body experience? Or is the person's mind manufacturing the perceptual stimuli needed to make these multiple views? I really don't know. I just know it happens.

METAPHYSICAL QUESTIONS ASIDE

The idea of a moving viewpoint may sound mystical, as if it were some sort of extrasensory perception. This phenomenon could be explained by any number of theories, including the quantum physics concept that perception itself produces effects on the object that is being perceived. Another explanation might be some form of perception that has not yet been identified, like the sonar that gives dolphins a three-dimensional mental image of their surroundings and even allows them to communicate these images to other dolphins. Or it could be conceived as a form of imagination, where the person mentally constructs multiple views of the object or symbol being perceived.

The simple fact is that the mind's eye does perceive multidimensionally, and learning to control its position does allow dyslexics to perceive two-dimensional symbols accurately. Thousands of people have improved their reading and writing skills by learning the techniques described in the following chapters.

If the idea of moving a mental viewpoint around in space sounds far-fetched to you, it's probably because you aren't dyslexic. When I first explain the concept to most dyslexics, they invariably say, 'That's exactly what I do!'

Individuals naturally place their mind's eyes in

various advantageous positions. Dancers and athletes (two favourite professions of dyslexics) ordinarily have their mind's eyes positioned above their bodies—a convenient vantage point.

Without getting into theoretical discussions about the nature of reality, let's just say that if a person subliminally causes the mind's eye to rove, he or she experiences that multidimensional perception as reality.

FINDING THE SWITCH

The dyslexic person needs to learn how to turn the disorientation switch on and off. This is accomplished by consciously positioning the mind's eye. When it is moved to a certain place, the person stops being disorientated and is able to perceive the outside or 'real' world correctly. The person becomes orientated.

The optimum position of the mind's eye for orientation was discovered through trial and error. It varies with the individual, and can change slightly over time, but it falls within a certain area. The location for orientation is a few centimetres to 30 centimetres above and behind the head, on the centreline of the body. A person who learns to move his mind's eye to what I call his 'orientation point' has learned to shut off the distorted perceptions of dyslexia.

The Davis Perceptual Ability Assessment described in Chapter 26 is used to determine whether a person has the ability to move the mind's eye around and see a mental image from different perspectives in space. In other words, can the person intentionally produce disorientation?

The Davis Orientation Counselling procedure described in Chapter 27 is used to teach the person how to control the position of the mind's eye and move it to the optimum viewpoint for real-world perception—especially for reading.

The goal of Orientation Counselling is *not* to stop the person from disorientating, for disorientation is a valuable talent. Orientation Counselling trains the person to turn disorientations on and off at will. With some practice, the mental on-off switch will become available, and the person will be able to use it easily.

CHAPTER 25

Implementing the Davis Procedures

This book is not intended to be a *self-help manual*, so a coach or helper is needed. The Orientation Counselling procedure is not designed as a 'read-it-and-do-it-to-yourself' exercise, because your attention would be too divided for the process to be effective. This process is one you would learn in order to help someone else. If you want to go through the process yourself, get someone else to read it and practise it, and then guide you through it. That way you can relax and just do it.

The procedures in the following chapters are all the basic methods that have successfully helped dyslexic adults and children since the opening of the Reading Research Council's Dyslexia Correction Center in 1982. In a Davis Orientation Counselling Programme these methods are implemented intensively, five to six hours per day, over the course of five days. Symbol Mastery on the trigger words is started during the programme, then completed at home with a parent, spouse or tutor. An intensive schedule has proved best for achieving fast and effective results. A schedule of just one hour a day or one hour per week is effective, but will require more total time because of the loss of momentum between sessions. Just doing 'bits and pieces' of the programme will fall short of the overall goal of really correcting dyslexia.

A good way to become comfortable with the procedures is to practise them aloud with a friend or act them out by yourself. Go through the explanations and draw the steps on a piece of paper while gathering imaginary answers.

AM I QUALIFIED TO DO THIS?

If you are literate and sincerely want to help someone overcome reading, writing and studying problems, the answer is yes. Being willing to spend some time giving a student individual attention and positive feedback is the main prerequisite for using these procedures. Teachers should simply treat them as exercises. They are not harmful. If done wrong, they may at worst produce mild dizziness which a short walk or nap will relieve. Parents may find these procedures difficult only if they do not first have their child's willingness to participate, or use any pressure or coercion.

SMALL CHILDREN VS. OLDER DYSLEXICS

Orientation Counselling and Symbol Mastery are two complementary but different procedures. Orientation Counselling corrects perception; Symbol Mastery corrects dyslexia.

Symbol Mastery has also been found to be a useful addition to many curricula for enhancing creativity and language skills. Children under the age of seven or eight (depending on the child's maturity level) are generally better off starting with Symbol Mastery. Younger children can be taught the basic numerals and the alphabet by building them in clay. Using Symbol Mastery with early reading schemes has the added benefit of teaching the meanings of words. Children don't have to be dyslexic to use this learning method—it works for all of them. They enjoy it, too!

Later, children who develop dyslexic symptoms can be taught Orientation when they are ready— somewhere between the ages of seven for early developers and nine for late developers.

As a general rule, most dyslexics aged eight or over should start with Orientation Counselling, because they are already experiencing the frustration of not being able to read, write or spell well. Part of the gift of dyslexia is the tendency to disorientate spontaneously when confused. This way of thinking is on automatic pilot for the dyslexic, and needs to be brought under conscious control. Orientation Counselling will enable the person to perceive accurately and consistently when dealing with language and communication.

THE ORDER OF THE PROCEDURES

Start with the Perceptual Ability Assessment. This will tell you if the person is a candidate for the rest of the methods. You should also interview the person to find out what areas of difficulty he or she wishes to improve. Even if you think you already know what the person wants help with, it is a good idea to ask anyway. This allows the problem to be expressed. Parents are often surprised to discover that reading is not at all important to their child, whereas 'playing football better' or 'making friends' *is* important. By being creative, a parent or teacher can help a child do both better using the Davis methods.

Once you know the student can create mental images and move his or her mind's eye with no problem, the next step is the Orientation Counselling session (Chapter 27). Follow this with a reading exercise from Spell-Reading (Chapter 32) appropriate to the person's reading ability. This provides immediate practice in detecting and correcting disorientations. As needed, do Release (Chapter 28) to prevent 'holding' and headaches.

After the Orientation session, you are ready to implement the Basic Symbol Mastery steps detailed in Chapter 31.

For the next two or three days, do Review (Chapter 28) with your student at the beginning of the day to ensure the orientation point is in the correct place. On the third or fourth day, do Fine Tuning (Chapter 29).

Alternate Symbol Mastery with the Spell-Reading exercises as you proceed. Once the student has mastered all the basic language symbols, proceed to words. When he or she is familiar and comfortable with doing Symbol Mastery on words (Chapter 33), the entire list of small words should be mastered. This is best done over several months, two to three definitions at a time.

TIPS FOR SYMBOL MASTERY

Treat this procedure as an adventure and a game, not as work. The student should have a desire to improve his or her ability to use written language. You might want to have a discussion about the benefits of being able to read.

Avoid criticising the artistic qualities of the student's clay creations or correcting them yourself. To encourage accuracy and self-correction, prompt with statements like these:

'Check and see if that letter is the same as the example.'

'If you weren't going to say anything or use your hands, would the clay say it all?'

'I don't quite see it. Can you show it more clearly?'

'What is it you want to show?'

'Are you satisfied with the way that looks?'

When students first start learning the Symbol Mastery techniques, they may not fully grasp the concept as their own. They may need to repeat the steps on a particular word or concept. But once they are in the groove, mastering a definition once is enough.

Rote repetition or testing the student is not necessary. Once something is done correctly, it's finished. Praise the student and go on to something else. Trust the process to work. The proof will come in the form of increased self-esteem, greater desire to read and progressive improvement in study skills.

You can master the words on the small word list randomly, in any order, coming back to fill in alternative definitions. One of the gifts of dyslexia is the ability to sort things out automatically. Take advantage of it. Take frequent breaks, just for a few minutes. This lets the knowledge sink in and prevents boredom.

Keep it fun and adventurous. That is the best way to encourage real learning.

CHAPTER 26

Perceptual Ability Assessment

What follows is the assessment procedure as taught in Davis Orientation Mastery Workshops. It is designed to determine whether a person with a learning disability or other perceptual problem is a candidate for Orientation Counselling. We use this assessment for children and for adults. We do not ordinarily make the assessment on children until the age of seven, because that is when the symptoms of dyslexia typically begin to manifest.

The assessment is arranged in the form of a script, but there is no need to follow any rote procedure once you have a sense of what you are after.

Anyone with the unique perceptual abilities of a dyslexic should be able to do this exercise easily. Pun intended, it should be a piece of cake for them.

However, if a person is obviously dyslexic, yet can't perceive a mental image as requested, there is probably an 'old solution' blocking the picture-making or seeing process (see Chapter 5). In such a case, contact a Davis Dyslexia Association affiliate for advice and assistance. Stress, physical illness and certain medications can also inhibit mental perceptions.

DAVIS PERCEPTUAL ABILITY ASSESSMENT

1 Greeting and Introduction

Greet the person and introduce yourself. As appropriate, explain the nature of the assessment.

2 Concept Clarification

What to say	What to do
Are you right-handed or left-handed?	*Make a note of the answer for future reference.*
What I am interested in is your imagination. Mainly that part of your mind where you can close your eyes and make a picture of something and see the picture. Does that make sense to you?	*If 'yes', continue. If 'no', explain further by asking him to imagine something he likes with his eyes closed. If the person can't form a mental (imaginary) image, stop.*

What to say	What to do
	Draw two circles on a blank piece of paper.

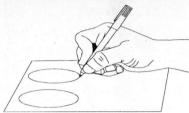

What to say	What to do
This circle represents you.	*Point to one of the circles.*
This represents me.	*Point to the other circle.*
If you are looking at me, you are looking *from* here.	*Tap your pencil on the first circle.*
And you are looking *to* or *at* me over *here*.	*Draw an arrow from the first 'you' circle to the second 'me' circle.*
As long as we are looking with our eyes, we know exactly where we are looking from. But what about when we are looking at a picture with our minds?	*Point at your own eyes.* *Pause for a second.*
We are doing the same thing. We are looking *at* something —*from* some place.	*Point at the 'me' circle as you say 'at'. Point at the 'you' circle as you say 'from'.*
I want to call the place we look from the MIND'S EYE because it is what sees when we are imagining. It is what is doing the looking.	*Make sure he gets the idea.*

What to say	What to do
Do you like cake?	NOTE: *Most people like cake, so in this example, we'll assume they do. If 'no', try pie, pizza or any distinctly-shaped object that the person can imagine easily.*
What kind of cake is the best kind?	*Note what kind of cake he likes for future reference.*

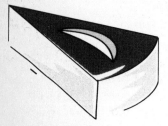

3 Assessment	*Have the person sit directly in front of you, close enough for you to be able to reach over and touch his forehead without getting out of your chair, but not so close as to make him feel uncomfortable.*
Is it all right if I touch your hands in what we are going to do?	*Get his consent.*
We are going to use both of your hands, so I need you to keep them available for me.	*Take the person's opposite-to-handedness hand (if right-handed take his left hand; if*

What to say	*What to do*

left-handed take his right). Position the hand, palm up, about where he would hold a book when reading.

Let's imagine a piece of _____ cake is sitting right here in your hand. Tell me when you've got it.

'Imagine a piece of chocolate cake in your hand.' (Tap the palm.)

Describe the cake just as he described it, using his exact words: 'A big slice of Black Forest gâteau' or 'sponge cake with green icing'.

'Close your eyes.'

Close your eyes. I want you to keep your eyes closed until I tell you to open them, OK?

Make the request when he says he has a mental picture (if his eyes aren't already closed).

NOTE: *If the person cannot visualise an object or has difficulty maintaining the image, you can either stop or*

What to say	What to do

attempt to coach the person into creating a mental image. Difficulty in visualising indicates that Orientation Counselling will not be easy for the person.

By asking simple questions, determine how the imaginary object is positioned in the hand. Continue until you also have a clear mental image of it sitting in the person's hand.

If you cannot make a visual copy of the imaginary object, at least get a sense of its size, shape, and position.

Take the index finger of the other hand between your thumb and middle finger. Raise the finger to a point a few centimetres from the forehead, on a level just slightly above eye level.

I want you to shift your imagination and put your mind's eye *here*, where your finger is, and look at the piece of cake from *here*.

Tap the tip of his index finger with your index finger as you say 'here'.

What to say	What to do

It's as if you have risen a little to get another view of the cake from *here*.

Tap the finger again. Wait several seconds . . .

Can you see the cake from *here*?

Tap the finger again.

NOTE: *If the person cannot make this first shift easily, do not continue. Go to step 4, ending the assessment. Explain that the assessment is over and that Orientation Counselling is not indicated.*

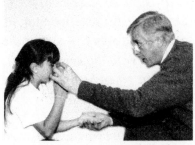

'Look at the piece of cake from here.' (Tap the finger.)

I want you to keep your mind's eye in your finger. Now I'm going to move your finger. I want your mind's eye to move with it, OK?

NOTE: *Do not move the finger while giving instructions or talking to the subject. Make your statement* before *starting to move the finger and* stop *moving the finger before you begin talking again.*

Move the finger slowly and smoothly to a position part way round the open hand. Keep the finger about the same distance from the open hand as the person's eyes are.

What to say	What to do
Can you see the cake from *here*?	*Tap the finger.*

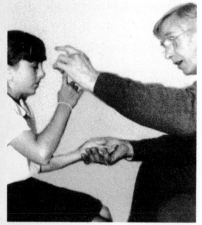

'Can you see the piece of cake from here?'

When 'yes', ask questions that require a verbal response. Pay attention to response time, variations in speech patterns and any manifestations of confusion or disorientation. Once you are satisfied that the person has actually shifted the mind's eye to the new position, you can go to Step 4 and end the assessment at any time.

If you are not sure whether the person has actually moved the mind's eye, go to the next step.

I am going to move your finger again. I want your mind's eye to move with your finger, OK?

Move the finger slowly and smoothly a little farther round the open hand. Don't move the finger more than a quarter of the distance round, above or below the open hand during any one move.

Can you see the piece of cake from *here*?

Tap the finger again.

When 'yes', again ask questions, looking for indications that the person actually has moved the mind's

What to say	*What to do*
	eye. He should see a mental (imaginary) picture from the perspective of his fingertip, as if he were looking at the object from that position.
	Repeat this process of moving the mind's eye and questioning until you are satisfied the mind's eye has actually been moved.

4 Ending the Assessment

I want you to put your mind's eye back in the place where it was when we first started. I want you to get your original view of that piece of cake.	*Slowly and smoothly move the finger towards the eye on the handedness side of the person's body. When within a few centimetres of the eye, stop the finger.*
Take your mind's eye out of your finger and get your original view of the cake—from your eyes.	
	Wait several seconds.
Do you have your original view?	*When 'yes', move the finger in the direction of the lap and release the finger.*

What to say	What to do
Make the piece of cake go away, and tell me when it is gone.	NOTE: *If he has any difficulty making the object disappear, have him do a 'reverse blink' by rapidly opening and shutting his eyes.*
	When it is gone, touch the palm of the open hand.
Put another piece of cake here in your hand and tell me when you have it.	NOTE: *The reason for forming a second image and make it disappear is to ensure the mind's eye has returned to its original location so that the person will not remain disorientated.*
Make this piece of cake go away and when it is gone, open your eyes.	*When his eyes open, move the open hand towards the lap and release it.*

CHAPTER 27

Turning It Round

If the person has dyslexia, the process of correcting it begins with getting the perceptual distortions under control. This means learning how to turn the disorientations *on* and *off* intentionally. The symptoms of dyslexia are the symptoms of disorientation, so once the dyslexic knows how to turn the disorientations off, he or she can also turn the symptoms off.

Once the disorientations are turned off, the person will stop creating dyslexia symptoms. It may seem that the problem is solved, but orientation is merely the first step of the correction process.

It usually takes less than an hour to put someone through the initial session of Davis Orientation Counselling. At the end of a successful session, with some help at catching disorientations as they occur, the dyslexic's reading skill is usually dramatically improved. It can appear that some kind of magic or miracle has just happened, but actually you are only seeing the person's real skills without the interference of disorientations. We have documented cases where the reading ability of teenagers has improved immediately by as many as eight age levels, as a result of Orientation Counselling alone.

It would be easy to believe that something that could produce such a dramatic effect must be difficult to learn. In fact, it is very easy for dyslexics to learn. This is because they already know how to do it. They have been doing it since they were a few months old. They just weren't consciously aware of what they were doing all along. Orientation Counselling enables them to understand a skill they already have and gives them a means to control it.

The procedure that follows may sound like a visualisation exercise when you read it. Yet when properly applied, it can produce near-miraculous results. There are only a few rules to follow.

1   Make sure the person is a candidate for Orientation Counselling by evaluating her ability to move the mind's eye with the assessment described in the last chapter.

2   Make sure the person wishes to perform the process. She must be willing and eager to do it. We generally do not perform this process on children younger than seven, because they haven't yet recognised disorientation as a problem at school. As far as they're concerned, nothing needs putting right.

3 Maintain a friendly, supportive control as you guide the person through the steps. She shouldn't have to think about what she is doing, but should simply follow the instructions.

4 Ensure the person is not tired, hungry or taking any medications that interfere with perception or thought.

What follows is a script of an initial Davis Orientation Counselling session as done at the Reading Research Council. Correctly performed, it has produced a 97 per cent success rate. If you don't get results, it's likely that one of the four rules listed above has not been followed.

As with the Perceptual Ability Assessment, you are encouraged to use your own words.

DAVIS ORIENTATION COUNSELLING
INITIAL SESSION PROCEDURE

---

1 Greeting and Introduction

Greet the person and establish a rapport. As appropriate, explain the goal and objective of the procedure as stated at the beginning of this chapter.

2 Concept Clarification

If you do not have the notes made during the assessment, you must establish the handedness of the person, and determine an object he or she can imagine easily. Otherwise, use the same piece of cake or object that was used in the initial assessment.

Explain the concept of orientation as 'putting yourself in the proper position in relation to the true facts and conditions of your surroundings'.

Explain that disorientation is a condition in which the brain is not receiving what the eyes see or what the ears hear; the balance and movement sense is altered, and the time sense is either speeded up or slowed down.

What to say	What to do
Before we start the session, I am going to go over everything we are going to do. I will show you on paper first, then we'll do it step-by-step. OK?	*Get a piece of paper and have the person sit so that the paper can be clearly seen.*

'I'll draw for you exactly what we're going to do so you'll know what to expect.'

What to say	What to do

There are two reasons why we are going over this first. One is to let you know what will be happening so that there won't be any surprises. The other is to make sure you understand what I will be asking you to do.

Write on the paper the person's name, your name, the date, the name of the process, the object to be used in visualisation, and the handedness of the person.

I do ask you not to do any of the process while I'm showing you on the paper. That would only create confusion. Just watch and listen. If you have a question, ask. After we finish going over it on the paper, I will walk you through it step-by-step. OK?

Draw two circles on the paper. Make one circle a 'top view' of a head. Make the other circle a 'side view' of a head.

These are two views of the same head, looking down at it from the top and from the side.

As in the assessment, we'll have you imagine a piece of _____ in your hand.

Draw the object (the piece of cake used in the assessment) to be visualised in front of both views. On the side view the object should be below eye level at about a 45° angle from the line of sight.

What to say	What to do

Then we will have you shift your imagination and put your mind's eye in your finger, off to the side, and have you look at the piece of cake from *here*.

Put an X on the person's 'handedness' side of the top view to indicate the position of the mind's eye (to the right if the person is right-handed).

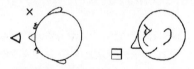

Draw a straight line from the object through the top view. Extend the line well past the back of the head. On the side view, draw a straight line from the object, through the end of the nose, through the head, and extend the line well past the top back of the head.

Once your mind's eye is in your finger, we will have you imagine a line that goes from the piece of cake straight through your head. The line will go from the piece of cake into your nose, through your head, and will stick up about 30 centimetres or so above and behind your head.

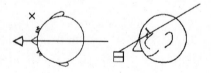

What to say	**What to do**

After you have drawn that line in, we will have you move your mind's eye round so it's a few centimetres above and behind your head and we'll have you position it on the line. OK?

Make an X on each of the lines going through the heads.

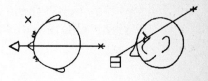

Do you know how an anchor for a boat works?

You have a heavy weight, and you attach a line or chain to it. You attach the line to the boat and throw the anchor into the water. The anchor sinks into the mud or hooks on a rock or something and when the line is pulled tight it keeps the boat from moving. Right?

Be sure the concept of 'anchor line' is understood.

We are going to use the same idea as an anchor. When your mind's eye is in the right place on the line above and behind your head, we are going to have you put an anchor line down to the top of each of your ears, and anchor it in. Then we'll have you put a third anchor line down to the

What to say	What to do

top of your head and anchor it in there. Then we'll have you pull the three anchor lines tight and attach them together right where your mind's eye is.

Draw the three anchor lines on the paper as you explain it.

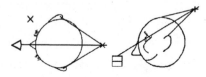

Any questions so far?

Once the three anchor lines are drawn in, we won't need the line that goes down to the piece of cake any more, so you'll rub it out and it will be gone. We won't need the piece of cake any more either so we'll have you rub that out also.

To simulate rubbing out, draw a wavy line over one of the long lines and the object at its end.

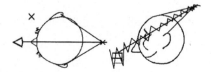

What you will have left are the three anchor lines that come together and make a point above and behind your head.

What to say	What to do

Draw three lines coming together, separately on another part of the paper. Draw a circle around the intersecting point.

We are going to call the place where the lines come together an ORIENTATION POINT. It is the PLACE where the lines end. We call the lines anchor lines, not to anchor the mind's eye there, which you can't do anyway, but to anchor this place there so it is in the same place all the time.

Any questions so far?

What we are really after is a group of brain cells down in the middle of the brain that are responsible for disorientation. When those brain cells are turned *off*, our brain gets exactly what our eyes see, as our eyes are seeing it; and our brain gets exactly what our ears hear, as our ears are hearing it. Our balance and movement sense is accurate, and our sense of time is accurate. When those brain

What to say	What to do

cells are turned *on*, our brain doesn't get what our eyes see; it gets what we think our eyes are seeing. Our brain doesn't get what our ears hear; it gets what we think our ears are hearing. Our balance and movement sense changes and our internal sense of time can either speed up or slow down. What we really need is the OFF-SWITCH for those brain cells. That's what that orientation point is. It's the off-switch for the disorientation.

The way we switch the off-switch *off* is simply by putting the mind's eye on that orientation point. That turns those brain cells off.

Draw an X inside the circle where the three separate lines come together.

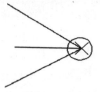

If our mind's eye is sitting in this spot, the brain cells are turned off. But if something happens that can cause a disorientation, the mind's eye doesn't stay there, it moves.

Draw three additional lines coming together, and put an X on the point.

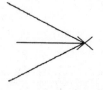

What to say	**What to do**

So it takes off, and we are disorientated. In the past, if we waited long enough, or if we went for a walk, or did something other than what we were doing that caused the disorientation, eventually our mind's eye would come back, and we would be all right again—until something else caused another disorientation.

Draw an arrow from the point going off to the side.

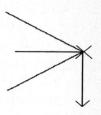

When we have an orientation point, we can deliberately bring the mind's eye back, put it on the point, and end the disorientation. We don't have to wait, or do something else, or torture ourselves. Simply putting the mind's eye back in that place turns off the disorientation. It also turns off the feeling of confusion and stops the mistakes.

Draw a line back to the point and retrace the X.

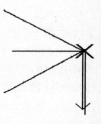

Any questions so far?

Draw three more lines that come together; they should be longer and bolder than the others.

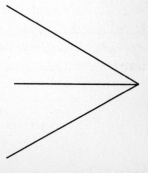

What to say	What to do

Of course, we can't see a mind's eye. In fact, it can't even see itself in a mirror. It is invisible. So we'll just imagine for a moment that this thing is a mind's eye. OK?

Pick up some small object (a coin is fine), and hold the object so that the person can see it.

When we get to the part of the session where you have put the three anchor lines in, your mind's eye will be sitting exactly where they come together.

Position the object on the drawing, exactly where the three lines come together.

For the first time in your life, you will have deliberately turned off the brain cells that cause disorientation. The only problem is that we don't learn very much from doing something just once.

So when we have your mind's eye sitting on that point, we are going to find some real-life thing that can cause your mind's eye to jump off the point, and disorientate you.

Knock the object off the point where the lines come together.

What to say	What to do

When that happens, I'll stop you from looking at the thing that made it jump, and have you simply put your mind's eye back on the point.

Put the object back on the point where the lines come together.

That will turn off the disorientation. The confusion will go away. Then I'll show you what made it happen.

Then we'll find another thing that will make it jump.

Knock the object off the point, and put it back again.

You'll put your mind's eye back, I'll show you what made it jump, and then we'll do it again. We'll do it again and again, until you are an expert at putting your mind's eye back on your orientation point. You will be able to do it quickly, easily, and know that you did it.

What you will have then is the ability to turn off a disorientation. It won't matter what turned it on, the action of simply putting your mind's eye on your orientation point will turn it off. Any questions?

What to say	What to do
There is one more point we need to make.	
We call this a *line*, because it has length to it. Just like this pen/pencil has length to it. But what about when we are looking down the length of it?	*Point to one of the anchor lines on the drawing.* *Pick up your pen or pencil.* *Point the end of the pen/pencil towards the eyes of the person.*
It doesn't look long at all, does it? It looks like a dot, doesn't it?	
If the mind's eye were sitting right *here*, it wouldn't see the three lines as lines at all, would it?	*Point to a place on the drawing where the three lines come together as you say 'here'.*
It would see them as three dots, or as one dot if they were pushed together. Do you agree?	*Draw one dot, and also three dots touching each other.*
Do you have any questions about what we are going to do?	
If you don't have any (more) questions, let's do it!	

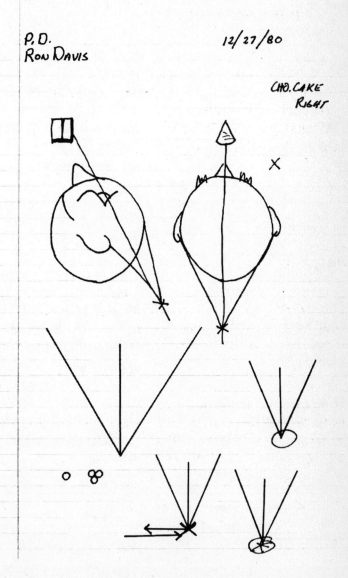

Your diagram for explaining a Davis Orientation Counselling session will look something like this when you have finished.

What to say	**What to do**
3 Process Sequence	
	Have the person sit directly in front of you, close enough for you to be able to reach over and touch her forehead without getting out of your chair. Do not sit so close to the person that you make her feel uncomfortable.
Is it all right if I touch your hands in what we're going to do?	*Get consent.*
We are going to use both of your hands, so I need you to keep them available for me.	*Take the person's opposite-to-handedness hand (if right-handed take her left hand; if left-handed take her right). Position the hand, palm up, approximately where a book would be held for reading.*
Let's imagine a piece of _____ cake is sitting right here in your hand. Tell me when you've got it.	*Describe the cake exactly as it was described to you in the assessment.*
Close your eyes. I want you to keep your eyes closed until I tell you to open them, OK?	*When you are certain the person has formed a mental image and her eyes are closed, take the index finger of the other (handedness) hand*

What to say	What to do

| | *between your thumb and middle finger. Raise the finger to a point off to the side of the forehead on eye level (where you placed the X beside the head on the initial drawing).* |

I want you to shift your imagination and put your mind's eye *here* . . . where your finger is, and look at the piece of cake from *here*.

Tap the index finger with your index finger as you say 'here'.

It's the same as if you have leant over and are looking from *here*.

Tap the finger again. Wait several seconds.

Can you see the piece of cake from *here*?

Tap the finger. When 'yes', go to the next step.

Imagine a straight line that goes from the piece of cake into your nose, through your head, and sticks up about 30 centimetres behind you. Draw that line in, and tell me when you have it there.

Confirm that the line is there.

I am going to move your finger. I want your mind's eye to move with it, OK?

NOTE: Do not move the finger while giving instructions or talking to the person. Finish making your statement before starting to move the finger and stop moving the finger before you begin talking again.

What to say

I want to put your mind's eye on the line above and behind your head, so let me move your finger. Let your mind's eye move with it.

Stop the finger 15 to 25 centimetres above and behind the head.

I can't see the line. Only you can see it, so I need you to make the fine adjustment to get the mind's eye right on it.

What to do

You will need to stand up to reach above and behind the person's head. Do so quietly and gently.

Move the finger s l o w l y and s m o o t h l y in a direction towards the midline of the body above and behind the head. Stop the finger about 15 to 25 centimetres above and behind the head.

If the person's elbow is sticking out to the side of her body, you may need to turn her shoulder so that the elbow points forward. This way the hand can easily reach above and behind the head.

Loosen your grip on the index finger, and allow the person to move the finger freely. It may take the person several seconds to find the exact spot. When the person stops moving the finger, grasp it again.

What to say	What to do

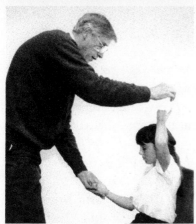

Look to see that the finger is on what would be the midline of the body (it seldom is).

If it is on midline, go to the next step.

'I'll need you to make the final adjustment to get your mind's eye right on the line.'

[It seems to be a bit off to the side. Is it all right if I move it just a bit?]

[If it is not on midline, without changing the distance from the head, move the finger to midline.]

Pull the line to come to *here* and tell me when you've got it.

Tap the finger.

'Pull the line to here.' (Move the finger to the midline and tap it.)

What to say	What to do

Can you see your ears from *here*? You can see right through your hair.

Tap the finger.

When 'yes', go to the next step.

[If 'no', have the person 'feel' where the ears would be. If necessary have her feel her ears with her hand (use the hand holding the imaginary object). If feeling them does not bring about seeing them, have the person imagine where her ears would be and make a mental picture of them.]

Put anchor lines down to the top of each ear, anchor them in, and pull them tight to *here*.

Tap the finger.

Put another anchor line down to the top of your head, anchor it in and pull it tight to *here* as well.

Tap the finger.

Attach the three lines together.

Confirm that this is done.

I want to move your finger, but I don't want your mind's eye to come with it this time. OK?

Get agreement.

What to say	What to do

As I move your finger, leave your mind's eye at the end of the lines.

Move the finger to the side a few centimetres.

Did your mind's eye stay on the lines?

If 'yes', move the finger over the shoulder in the direction of the lap. Release the finger and sit back down.

[If 'no', take the finger back to the position on the lines.]

[Take your mind's eye out of your finger and leave it on the lines when I move your finger.]

[Repeat this step until the mind's eye remains on the lines.]

We don't need the line that goes down to the piece of cake any more, so rub it out and tell me when it is gone. We also don't need the piece of cake any more, so rub it out and tell me when it is gone.

What colour are the three anchor lines you just put in?

Make a note for your reference.

Move your mind's eye to the place where the three (colour) lines come together. Tell me when it is there.

What to say	What to do
Do you see three dots, or one?	*Make a note.*
Are they the same colour as the lines?	*Make a note.*

What your mind's eye sees at this moment is what it should see when it is on the orientation point. Whenever you want to, you can look with your mind's eye. If it sees what it sees now, you know it is on the orientation point.

If it doesn't see what it sees right now, you would know that it isn't on the orientation point and you would have to move it to the point to see what it sees now. Any questions?

Open you eyes. Did it move when you opened your eyes?

If 'no', go to the next step.

[If 'yes', tell her to put it back.]

[Put it back.]

[If 'I don't know', have her close her eyes and check.]

[Close your eyes and look.]

The anchor lines put in by the dyslexic during Davis Orientation Counselling will converge at a point 15 to 25 centimetres above and behind the head. It will be at approximately a 45° angle, precisely on the midline of the body.

What to say	What to do

4 Explanation

I can't see your mind's eye. I can't see your anchor lines. If I hadn't been here while you were doing this, I wouldn't even know that you have them. If I can't tell, nobody else can tell either, so only you know for sure. You don't have to be concerned that anybody will think you are weird or that you are doing something that they can't do.

You can't touch a mind's eye; nothing can.

You don't have to worry about anything hitting it; or knocking it into a wall, a door or anything else. You don't have to worry about catching it in the car door. It goes right through things, as if they weren't even there.

Wave your hand above and behind your head.

'*You don't have to worry about knocking your mind's eye off or anyone seeing your lines.*'

When your mind's eye is sitting on the point, it is located by the lines that go to your ears and the top of your head. You can't move fast enough to lose it. You can't turn your head

What to say	What to do

fast enough to knock it off. It just sits there and goes where your head and ears go.

Any questions?

Do you know what the word 'responsibility' means?

Whether 'yes' or 'no', get the following concept across.

Let me give you a (simple/ simpler) definition. Responsibility is the ability and the willingness to control something. Control in its simplest form is the ability to cause something to change, or to cause it not to change.

Because I can reach over and move your hand, I am changing something about your body. That change is happening, and you're not doing it. I am responsible for that change. You aren't, because you didn't do it. Right?

Take one of the person's hands and move it a bit.

But I can't reach over and move your mind's eye. No one can. There isn't a person, animal, machine or anything on this earth that can move

What to say	What to do

your mind's eye one billionth of a millimetre. But you can put it anywhere you want to. That means that you have total control, which also means that you have total reponsibility for where you mind's eye is and what it does.

Do you agree?

That also means that when it jumps, when you get disorientated, you are the one who made it jump. When you were very young, you set it up so that whenever you were confused enough, your mind's eye would automatically go off and try to get rid of the confusion. When the confusion was about a real object it actually worked. It would get rid of the confusion. But it won't work with a symbol, and all words are symbols, so it won't work with words. Moving the mind's eye around just creates more confusion.

Now you have a problem. Your mind's eye jumps every

What to say	What to do

time you get confused, and you don't want it to do that any more.

The problem is, it is still going to jump. If you try to hold it on the point to keep it from jumping, while at the same time you are automatically trying to make it jump, you are going to get a headache.

The only solution I know is to go ahead and let it jump. When it does, simply bring it back. That will be your job, your responsibility. Whenever it jumps, you put it back.

Do you have any questions?

Is your mind's eye still sitting on your orientation point?

If 'yes', go to the next step.

[If 'no', have her put it back.]

[Put it back on the point.]

For a little while, after we first get an orientation point, our mind's eye just floats around it. It doesn't just sit there. This happens to everyone. We call it 'drifting'.

What to say	What to do

As soon as you get used to controlling your mind's eye, putting it and leaving it on the orientation point, the drifting will stop. Then when you put your mind's eye there it will just sit there.

Don't try to hold your mind's eye there, just let it drift. Every once in a while, move it back to the point and let go of it. If you try to hold it there you are just prolonging the drifting phase.

Any questions?

5 Practising Using Orientation

Based on the disorientation history, select, an activity such as reading which will disorientate the person. Be alert for indications of disorientation. When a disorientation or mistake occurs, stop the activity.

Did your mind's eye move?

If 'no', continue the activity until it does.

[If 'I don't know', have her check.]

What to say	What to do

[Look with your mind's eye and see it sees the *(dot/dots)*.]

When it has moved, have her put it back.

Put it back.

Then point out the stimulus that triggered the disorientation.

Continue in this fashion until the person can quickly and easily put the mind's eye back on the orientation point, and sees that it makes a difference.

Point out each word that triggers a disorientation.

When the person can quickly and easily put the mind's eye on the orientation point, and knows that she has done so, the session is complete.

CHAPTER 28

Release and Review

As dyslexics develop orientation skills, it will become obvious to them that *if the mind's eye doesn't move, there are no mistakes.* As they become more aware of their state of orientation, they will notice that whenever their mind's eye moves, they disorientate. After they disorientate, they will either make a reading mistake, or some 'old solution' will automatically turn on.

It would seem that the next logical skill would be to develop a method of keeping the mind's eye on the orientation point. It is simple to do, and most students will try it. Unfortunately, this usually results in an intense headache.

The probable reason is that the mind's eye doesn't really move by itself. The student, on a subconscious level, is causing it to move. Moving it is an ingrained habit. Learning about orientation and the benefits of not moving the mind's eye won't prevent the student from making this natural reaction to confusion.

So when the student becomes confused, he or she will be attempting to move the mind's eye at the same time as trying to prevent it from moving—literally working against himself. We call this *holding*. It creates tension, which results in the headache.

Simply telling the student not to hold his mind's eye on the orientation point does not work. It's like telling him not to think about an elephant: it will cause him to do it instead of preventing it. The more he tries not to hold, the stronger the holding will become.

Besides, there is no reason why the student shouldn't disorientate when it's appropriate and useful.

A student who is holding the mind's eye rigidly on the orientation point will usually reach up and rub the back of his neck. When you see him do this, intervene with the *Release* procedure.

Signs of holding:

1   The student complains of a headache.

2   The student rubs or touches the back of the neck.

3   The skin tone becomes pale.

4   The brows wrinkle.

5   The student begins to look stressed or distressed.

RELEASE PROCEDURE

Have the student go through the Release procedure by reading or reciting these steps to him. As you go, make sure he performs the action requested before doing the next step. If he says he 'can't', or is not certain whether he has done a step, say, 'Imagine what it would be like to do that.'

Make a loose fist—not too tight. Just let your fingers curl into your palm. Now think the thought 'open hand', but, instead of opening your hand, make the fist tighter.

Think the thought again, 'open hand', and make the fist even tighter.

Again think the thought 'open hand', and make the fist really tight, really *really* tight, tight all the way up to your elbow.

Now without thought simply let your hand release. Let your entire hand go. Let your fingers find their natural place.

Feel the feeling that goes down your arm, through your hand all the way out to the tips of your fingers. That feeling is the feeling of *release*. When the word *release* is used, that feeling is what is meant.

The feeling of release is also the same feeling as the feeling of a sigh.

Do a sigh. Breathe in and hold it for a second or two. Then let the air rush out of your mouth, with a 'hunnnn' sound coming from your nose and throat.

A little sigh puts the feeling of release in your upper chest. A great big sigh can put that feeling all the way out to the tips of your fingers and toes.

Do a great big sigh. Get that feeling all through your body. Now let that feeling linger. Let that feeling remain in your body.

Now let your mind's eye have that feeling, by simply wanting it to. Your mind's eye can have that feeling. That's what your mind's eye should feel like.

Now have your mind's eye put that feeling down into your head and neck. You'll feel your neck muscles letting go. You'll feel them get loose.

> *If the student has a headache, use this step before continuing:*
>
> *Now have your mind's eye put that feeling right inside the headache. Have your mind's eye fill up the headache with the feeling of release. Have your mind's eye continue filling up the headache with release until it is completely gone.*

In the future, whenever you have to put your mind's eye back on the orientation point, after you've got it there let it go. Loose hold of it. It won't go anywhere, it'll just sit there. You don't have to hold it.

Every time you have to bring your mind's eye back, let it have that feeling of release. Then you won't have the headaches or the old solutions happening any more.

After the student has learned what release is and how to do it, there is no need to go through the whole procedure again. Simply ask or remind the student to 'do release' whenever you notice him holding, concentrating, tensing up, or exerting a lot of effort.

ORIENTATION REVIEW PROCEDURE

After a few hours, the orientation point established in the initial Orientation Counselling session may change location. As a result, from time to time you may need to check and see if it has moved, and if so, put it back to its original place. This is done with the Orientation Review procedure.

Simply ask the student to put his finger *where his orientation point is*. Typically when I do it, I say: 'Earlier when we did the orientation session, you got something called an orientation point. It's the place where the three lines make the point. Can you put your finger where that point is?'

When he does, check to see that his finger is on the

The right place.

Her mind's eye is too low and off to the right.

midline of his body and between 15 and 25 centimetres above and behind the head. If he puts his finger in the right place say: 'That's good. Keep using that point and everything should be all right.'

If he puts his finger anywhere other than in the right place, simply ask if you can do a 'slight adjustment'. (No one has ever said 'no'.)

Grasp his finger between your thumb and middle finger and gently pull it to the midline of the body. Tap the end of his finger with your index finger and say: 'Pull the point to here by adjusting the lines. Tell me when you've got it here.' Tap the finger again.

When he tells you that the point is now where you want it, tell him: 'That's good. Use this point, and everything should be all right.'

If the point continues to shift excessively after doing the above adjustment, tell the student to *'set the lines so they won't move'*.

Use Orientation Review only until you do the

Adjust the point and lines to the midline.

Fine Tuning procedure covered in the next chapter. After doing Fine Tuning, this method of checking the location of the orientation point is no longer appropriate.

CHAPTER 29

Fine Tuning

The Fine Tuning procedure is a method by which the orientated dyslexic can find his or her *optimum orientation point*. It is named after the process used to fine-tune a radio, moving the knob back and forth until the best possible reception is found.

The same thing can be done with the mind's eye. By moving it around the existing orientation point, the optimum place for orientation can be located.

There are several things to keep in mind here. The Fine Tuning procedure is best done after the orientated dyslexic has had at least two days' experience at controlling orientation. Fine Tuning should not be attempted until any and all drifting (slight floating of the mind's eye) has stopped.

During Fine Tuning the mind's eye can move in all directions, not just back and forth. Also, whenever the mind's eye is moving, a person will feel out of balance. Fine Tuning is done by moving it just a little, stopping it, and checking how things feel.

There are two ways students can tell when they have reached their optimum orientation place. First, the students will be perfectly balanced. They can stand on one foot without any movement in their foot, ankle, knee, hips or torso. They can hold that position until their muscles become physically tired. At that point, they can still remain comfortably balanced by simply switching to the other foot. Secondly, when their mind's eye is at their optimum orientation place, students will experience a profound feeling of well-being—what I call the *comfort zone*. It will just 'feel right'.

Often while doing Fine Tuning, students will move their mind's eye through the comfort zone. When this happens, the feeling of well-being will 'wash' over them momentarily. They will probably smile and will look relieved. But if they don't stop their mind's eye at that exact location, the feeling will vanish as quickly as it occurred.

Assuming we start with the mind's eye above and behind the head, the observable phenomena of the relationship between the mind's eye and the body are:

1   If the mind's eye is left of midline, the body is out of balance to the left.

2   If the mind's eye is right of midline, the body is out of balance to the right.

3 If the mind's eye is too far back, even if on midline, the body is out of balance in the backward direction.

4 If the mind's eye is too far foward, even if on midline, the body is out of balance in the forward direction.

5 If the mind's eye is too low, the body is out of balance in the backward direction.

6 If the mind's eye is too high, the body is out of balance in the forward direction.

7 If the mind's eye is in front of the centreline of the body, (1) and (2) above reverse.

Using the above information, the student can find the optimum orientation point.

The student does the procedure by slowly moving and stopping the mind's eye within the general area of the existing orientation point. This is done until perfect balance is achieved, and he or she experiences an overall feeling of well-being.

FINE TUNING PROCEDURE

As in all these procedures, use your own words.

What to say	What to do

Explain the concept of fine-tuning a radio and how it can apply to finding optimum orientation.

I want you to keep your eyes open during what we're about to do, OK?

Find a location where there is a view that extends a long way. This can be looking out of a window. Have the student stand facing the view.

Put your mind's eye on your orientation point.

Have the student check to see that the mind's eye is on the orientation point.

Stand next to the student and point out a particular spot or point in the vista. The spot or point should not be below eye level.

'*Look at that picture up there.*'

What to say	What to do

With your eyes looking at that (spot/point), balance on one foot.

NOTE: *It does not matter which foot she balances on. She can switch feet if she wishes.*

Gently grasp the student by the shoulders, then release the grasp without moving your hands far from the shoulders.

'*Keep looking at it and balance on one foot.*'

'*Give it a push and see what happens.*'

Now push your mind's eye off your point in my direction, and see what it does to your balance. I won't let you fall.

[Give it a good push; I won't let you fall.]

If the student doesn't lean into you . . .

What to say	What to do

NOTE: It is important that the student feels the body go out of balance in the direction the mind's eye moves.

Put your mind's eye back on point, and put your foot down.

Locate another spot or point that is closer, about 45° below the line of sight. Direct the person's attention to the spot/point.

Tip your head forward, and look directly at the (spot/point). Now balance on one foot.

'Look at that penny I threw on the floor and balance on one foot.'

Now, just like fine-tuning a radio, move your mind's eye around, and find the place where your body is in perfect balance.

Remember, while your mind's eye is moving, your

NOTE: *this process takes as long as it takes. The student*

What to say	What to do

balance is out, so move it just a bit, stop it, and then check. You'll know when you've got it by the feeling that it has.

may not find optimum orientation on the first attempt.

Don't let her stop unless she is very close to, or has actually found, the optimum orientation place.

When the student has found optimum orientation, or is getting tired and is very close, use the following steps to end the process.

Hold your mind's eye exactly where it is, and put your foot down.

Hold your mind's eye exactly where it is and pull your (dot/dots) to where your mind's eye is. You're not moving the mind's eye; you're moving the point *to* the mind's eye.

Let your anchor lines set and get hard where they are, just as concrete sets and gets hard. That way your point will be exactly where it should be and won't be moving around.

Confirm that this is done.

Explain that the student should use this procedure at least once a day to make sure the orientation point is optimum. Explain that, from time to time, the optimum place changes location for reasons unknown, and the student must adapt to that change using this procedure.

After Fine Tuning, do not ask students to try to put their finger where the point is. They probably won't be able to find it, and asking them to do so will only create confusion.

Future Orientation Review is done by simply having the student look down and balance on one foot, showing you that the balance is there.

There is only one optimum orientation point where all sensory data are most accurate. However, there are other orientation locations, one or more for each of the senses, where that sense will be very acute. The one for balance is 60 centimetres or more directly above the head, or forward of the centre of gravity. When working with athletes and so on (anyone with excellent balance), make sure they are orientating above and behind the head and not directly above or in front of it. Having the student look down while checking should ensure this.

CHAPTER 30

Coordination

After the Fine Tuning process is completed, there is a fast and simple way to put an end to *left/right confusion* problems for good. This process also addresses the dyspraxia problem described in Chapter 11. We call it Koosh Ball Therapy because we use two light, furry toy balls made of rubber band material for the process. We don't recommend other balls like tennis balls or ping-pong balls, because they have a tendency to bounce out of the person's hands before they are able to grasp them.

You can start doing this periodically after Fine Tuning, described in the previous chapter.

Stand two to three metres away from the person (closer for small children). Start by telling the student to 'check your point'. When he is on point (orientated), ask him to balance on one foot. He can stand on either foot, and can switch feet at any time.

Hold both balls in one hand. With the student

comfortably balanced on one foot, say, 'Catch one ball in one hand and the other ball in the other hand.'

1   Underhanded, toss each ball one at a time. Toss gently, aiming about chest high. Each time you toss a ball, say, 'One in one hand, one in the other.'

2   When the student can easily catch a ball in either hand without losing his balance, repeat, 'One in one hand, one in the other.' Then toss both balls *simultaneously*. Aim for a position directly in front of the person on the midline of the body. If properly tossed, one ball will be on each side of the midline. Be sure to toss them so that they

'One in one hand, one in the other.'

can be easily caught. When the student catches both balls, praise him and do it again.

3 After a while, say, 'I am going to toss them both to one side of you. I want you to catch them without losing your balance.' Do this for each side so the student has to cross the midline with the other hand to catch both balls. Don't aim too far to the side, or you will cause the person to lose balance.

This exercise makes a good break activity while doing Symbol Mastery on the small words.

Crossing the midline.

CHAPTER 31

Basic Symbol Mastery

Earlier, I mentioned that confusion about the meanings of trigger words was the underlying cause of the disorientations that cause the symptoms of dyslexia. They are the most important culprits, but there are many other symbols that can cause disorientations as well. Most dyslexics will 'trigger' on some individual letters of the alphabet and on some punctuation marks. Some will trigger on some speech sounds, maths symbols and numbers.

Truly to correct the learning disability of dyslexia, all the triggering words and symbols must be learned so thoroughly that they are mastered.

Ideally, these exercises should be done individually with the student, at the student's pace. Breaks should be taken often, especially after a success.

If the student is experiencing difficulty, or overwhelming confusion and disorientation, a break from the activity is a must. It is usually a sure indication that an environmental, physical or emotional distraction is present, or an earlier confusion or disorientation was overlooked. Be sure to find out which, and remedy the cause before continuing.

Techniques that can also facilitate this process are:

1   The helper does the exercises and clay representations along with the student.

2   The student instructs or tests the helper in the materials just covered.

3   The helper takes turns with the student, making up sample sentences and usage examples.

The materials you will need are:

- 500 g to one kilo of modelling clay per person
- examples of upper and lower case alphabets (enlarge the examples on pp. 200 and 201 as a model)
- dictionary
- grammar book
- primers, readers, workbooks, magazines and other reading materials
- paper
- pencil
- tools for cutting and shaping the clay
- scissors
- clean-up materials—paper towels or baby wipes.

A B C D E F G H I
J K L M N O P Q R
S T U V W X Y Z

Here are the upper and lower case letters used for basic Symbol Mastery at the Davis Dyslexia Correction Center. They were specially designed for modelling in clay. Enlarge these pages by about 150 per cent on a photocopier, then cut out each copy into three strips. Tape them together to make long strips that look like these:

A B C D E F G H I J K L M N O P Q R S T U V W X Y Z

zyxwvutsrqponmlkjihgfedcba

zyxwvuts

rqponmlkji

hgfedcba

THE END OF THE ALPHABET SONG

After Orientation Counselling, Symbol Mastery is used to master the alphabet and punctuation.

We use a basic form of Symbol Mastery for letters and symbols. The process is simple; we just want the students to master the symbols so that they no longer trigger disorientations. We have them create each symbol in modelling clay, identify it, and learn its use. For the alphabet, we have them create each letter. We start with upper case letters, working from *A* to *Z*.

ALPHABET MASTERY PROCEDURE

1   Familiarise students with clay. Shaping. Cutting. Rolling.

2   At any sign of disorientation, always stop and politely ask the student: 'Check your orientation,' or 'Get your dot/dots.' Then resume.

3   Have the student make the upper case alphabet letters *A* to *Z* in forward order. Letters should be at least five centimetres high. Written examples of the letters should be nearby for the student to look at.

4   Ask the student, 'Whose alphabet is this?'

Repeat the question conversationally until the student says, 'It's mine.' Then ask the student, 'Why?' or 'How come?' until the student says 'Because I made it,' or 'Because I created it.'

5 Have the student check to see that all the letters are correctly positioned and sequenced, and similar in size. If any errors are found, have the student compare with the examples and correct them.

NOTE: When doing Symbol Mastery, **never:**

- *criticise the student's artistic ability*

- *point out specific mistakes. Have the student find them by comparing the clay alphabet and the written reference.*

6 Ask the student, 'Are you happy with your alphabet?' If not, ask what could be better, and have him correct it until he is happy with it.

7 Ask the student how many letters are in the alphabet. If unsure, have the student count them (s l o w l y). Repeat this activity until the student is absolutely certain there are 26.

8 Have the student slowly and deliberately touch and say the name of each letter in forward order.

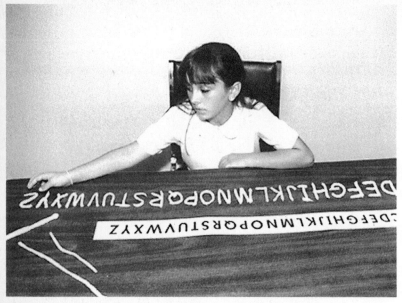

Touch and say the letters in both directions.

9 Have the student touch and say the name of each letter in backward order, starting from *Z*.

10 Note any errors, hesitations and confusions.

11 With letters that cause confusion or get mixed up, ask the student:

A 'Tell me something similar about these two letters.'

B 'Tell me something different about these two letters.'

Alternate asking questions (A) and (B) until there are no more answers.

For sequential errors or omissions, ask
(with student looking at the letter):

A 'What letter comes before _____?'
B 'What letter comes after _____?'

12   Have the student touch and say the letters forwards and backwards. Repeat until it becomes easy.

13   Have the student say the alphabet forwards, looking at the letters as needed.

14   Call out a letter of the alphabet, and have the student touch and say what letter comes before and after that letter. Do this until the student can easily and quickly find any letter in the alphabet.

15   Have the student say the alphabet backwards, taking as many 'peeks' as needed to get through it. Again, look for letters that cause problems, repeated looks and repeated confusions. Check for orientation and apply step (11) above to these letters as needed. Do this until the student can say the whole alphabet backwards at least once without looking.

16   If any signs of struggling or frustration appear, *BACK OFF* from this task. Take a short break. Then check orientation and go back to the step just preceding the one where trouble occurred. Repeat that step to a new success.

17 Continue to practise the alphabet backwards and forwards until the student knows it and can easily and comfortably recite it in both directions. Praise lavishly when this is accomplished. Always take a good break after this accomplishment.

18 Have the student make the alphabet in lower case manuscript backwards, *z* to *a*, in reverse

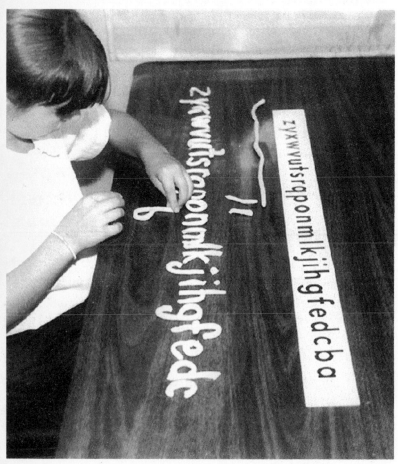

Lower case letters are made in reverse order.

order (but not with reversed letters). Use the examples on p. 201 as a model.

19 As above, monitor for problem letters, check orientation as needed, and have the student check for accuracy.

20 Have the student touch and say the letters in backwards order, *z* to *a*.

21 Now have the student recite the alphabet forwards. Watch for any signs of Alphabet Song, and slow the student down to say each letter separately and distinctly.

22 Randomly selecting any letter, ask the student what letter comes before and after it. Have the student peek, as needed, until he can comfortably tell you what letters come before and after every letter of the alphabet at random without looking.

Additional exercises that could be done here or later include:

- *Finding capital letters in the environment and naming them.*
- *Finding letter sections in the dictionary.*
- *Identifying letters in books.*
- *Finding letter sections in filing cabinets, phone books, encyclopedia, etc.*
- *Noticing different print styles and typefaces.*
- *Writing the letters.*

The work with the alphabet is complete when a student can recite the alphabet forwards and backwards with equal ease and speed, and can tell what letters come before and after every other letter in the alphabet. At this point, he knows the alphabet well enough not to be dependent on the Alphabet Song. There is no longer any need to sing it mentally, so the habit will disappear.

Next, we have the student go through the punctuation symbols. At first, it is more important for the dyslexic to know what to *do* when the marks are seen when reading aloud than to know how they are used in writing. This can be covered later.

PUNCTUATION MARKS MASTERY

1 Go over the definition of 'punctuation' from a simple dictionary.

2 Have the student make the period or full stop with clay.

3 Have the student write or copy the name of the mark on a small piece of paper (about 10 × 10 centimetres) after making each mark, and place the clay mark on the piece of paper in proper relation to what he has written. This can become a creative game. See opposite for a few examples.

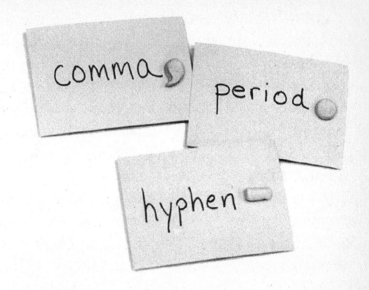

4 Point out each mark in various texts such as a primer, magazine, sign, etc. Also point out how each shape differs depending upon print style or typeface.

5 Have the student find the mark in various texts.

6 Referring to a grammar book or definition, go over the common usages of each mark. Emphasise what the student should *do* when he or she sees the mark while reading aloud. Halt for full stops, pause for commas, lilt the voice for question marks, and so on.

7 Have the student give verbal or written examples of how each punctuation mark is used.

8 Be sure the student knows how to pronounce the name of each mark.

9 Repeat steps 2–8 with the:

Question mark	Parentheses
Exclamation mark	Brackets
Comma	Ellipsis
Apostrophe	Asterisk
Dash	Colon
Hyphen	Semicolon
Quotation marks: double and single	Virgule or Slash

Because words are symbols that represent both sound and meaning, it is important that the student also be coached through all the speech sounds. This doesn't require a speech therapist, only the pronunciation key from any dictionary and a good coach.

If numbers are triggers for a student, the same basic process is done with numbers. All of this is completed before the trigger word list is started.

ADDITIONAL SYMBOL MASTERY EXERCISES

Pronunciation Mastery

1 Using a pronunciation key in a dictionary, demonstrate and practise how each of the letters is pronounced and made by the mouth, lips, and tongue.

2   Clarify each of the various symbols (diacritic marks) used in the pronunciation key, one at a time, using many examples.

3   Be sure to clarify the *schwa* sound and symbol.

4   Clarify what a syllable is, then practise finding them and counting them in some different words.

5   Clarify the use of accents and the accent symbols.

6   Find a word in a dictionary that the student has no idea how to pronounce. Have the student work out how to pronounce it using the pronunciation key—one syllable at a time, accenting correctly.

Print Styles and Typefaces

1   Using various texts, or ideally a book of printer's typefaces, point out some differences between the letters and numbers of varying typefaces.

2   Have the student find and point out some differences.

3   Have the student note the differences between the:

- lower case *a*, *g*, *q*, *t* and *y* from one print style to another.

- upper case *I* and lower case *l*.

- letters with and without serifs.

4   Be alert for disorientations, and always have the student correct them.

5   If needed, have the student make different types of letters in clay, and note similarities and differences.

6   Good examples and sources of differing print styles are phone book Yellow Pages, cartoon lettering, and newspaper and magazine advertisements.

Other Symbols

Mathematical, scientific, measurement, musical and other symbols which trigger disorientations can be addressed, clarified and mastered in the same manner as above.

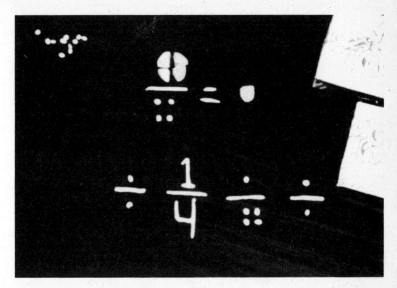

An example of how Symbol Mastery is used to represent the maths concept of the fraction ¼.

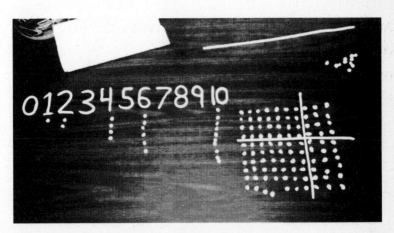

An example of how Symbol Mastery is used to show the meaning of the numerals 1, 2, 3, 4 and 10, and the concept of 7 × 4 = 28.

Kids' Stuff

Dan, who came for Orientation Counselling between his first and second years at secondary school, had an attitude typical of many dyslexic teenagers. He projected an air of exaggerated self-confidence and made the most of his natural ability to talk incessantly. He could have become a great salesman even if he had never done anything about his learning disability.

His initial Orientation Counselling session went well, and it was easy for him to maintain his orientation.

When we asked him to construct a clay alphabet, he had the same reaction as so many adults and teenagers: 'This is kids' stuff!' He grumbled, but went through the basic Symbol Mastery exercises and learned the alphabet backwards and forwards.

The first word from the trigger word list he chose to master was 'the'. To show the definition, he made a ball of clay and a model of a person pointing at it. Suddenly his face flushed, and his eyes filled with tears. He slammed his fist down on the table and said, 'Damn! Why didn't they teach me this at primary school? It's so simple!'

'I suppose they just didn't know how,' was the best answer I could come up with.

CHAPTER 32

Three Steps to Easier Reading

DYSLEXIC PERCEPTION AND CERTAINTY

Because dyslexic students' attention and awareness are widely spread out around the environment, they will naturally *look* at a word the same way they look at a tree in the park. They will see the entire tree at once. They don't first see the leaves on the left side, then the branches, then the trunk, then the branches and leaves on the right side. They just see the whole tree.

When dyslexic students learn to read while looking at entire words, they will always be guessing at what each word is, based on its overall appearance. Guessing will prevent the feeling of certainty they need to gain confidence in their reading ability.

These simple techniques were developed to enable non-readers to learn the most basic skills needed for comfortable reading, and to help dyslexics learn to read with ease and comprehension.

This process should be used fully after the student has completed Alphabet Mastery and Punctuation Mastery as described in Chapter 31. You can also use these techniques for the short reading session after you complete the last step of the Orientation Counselling session described in Chapter 27.

Begin using these techniques when the student starts to do Symbol Mastery on the small word list. It helps to vary the schedule and switch tasks occasionally. This prevents boredom.

1   SPELL-READING

The purposes of Spell-Reading are:

1　to train the student in left to right eye movement in reading

2　to enable the student to recognise letter groups as words.

A Spell-Reading session should be limited to a maximum of ten minutes, with breaks of the same length between sessions.

At this point, understanding what the student reads is of no concern. Your goal is only to get the student to recognise the letters in a word and then to repeat the word after you. This is not a phonics or a phonetic process, it is simply letter and word recognition. If the student has had previous instruction in sounding out words and attempts to do this, simply say, 'You don't need to sound out the word. Only say the name of the letters one at a time. All we want you to do is name the alphabet letters in the order they're written. Then you say the word after I say it.'

The Procedure

Spell-Reading trains the student's brain and eyes to scan from left to right while reading. Just as a computer must receive data in a proper sequence, the brain of the dyslexic needs the data in the order it was meant to be read. The proper sequence for reading in most languages is from left to right. Of course, this procedure can also be adapted for learning to scan the lines of a second language that is arranged from right to left, or from top to bottom.

Dyslexic students commonly have two reading habits that limit their ability:

1   Trying to go too fast.

2   'Working too hard' by concentrating heavily on the reading material.

These can be eliminated by Spell-Reading.

Before starting each session, tell the student, 'I want you to go slowly and easily. Being sure of what you're reading is more important than going fast.

Going slowly and easily will make this easy for you.'

Also you want the student to maintain orientation while Spell-Reading. Whenever a student makes an error or shows signs of concentration, have him check orientation. Just say, 'Check your point.' Naturally, you would omit this step for a student who hasn't had Orientation Counselling.

Adults vs. Children

With a child, use a primer or first reader for the process. Doing Spell-Reading with an adult works in the same way, but you'll need reading material that won't seem demeaning to the person. Use a simple text like this book or a newspaper. Even though this may be more difficult at first, there will be a bigger boost in self-esteem once the challenge is overcome.

Getting Started

Be sure the environment is comfortable and adequately lit for the student.

How the words are presented can vary, depending on the person's skill level. Most students can scan from one word to the next on a printed page. Others may be overwhelmed by the number of words they see at once. In this case, use a piece of paper to cover everything below the line the student is reading. Then use a second piece of paper to cover the right section of the line you are working on, so each word can be revealed one at a time by sliding the paper from left to right.

Sit facing the student with the reading material on the table between you. At the beginning of the session, tell the student: 'You spell the word. Then I will say the word. Then you say the word. If you suddenly know what the word is while you are spelling it, finish spelling it, then go ahead and say it without waiting for me.'

Present the words by pointing them out with your finger or a pencil, or revealing the words with sheets of paper as described above.

Insist that the student go slowly and easily.

It is your responsibility to catch the student's disorientations. Watch out for:

- substitution, omission or alteration of a letter
- moving the head closer to the page
- speech changes, such as hesitation, speeding up, slowing down, or reading in a flat, monotone voice
- rubbing the neck, fidgeting or wrinkling the eyebrows.

At the first sign of any disorientation, cover the material with your hand and ask the student to check orientation. If need be, take a short break.

Praise any and all improvement. Your praise is the student's reward. It will lift the student's self-esteem.

During this exercise, a point will be reached when

the student recognises many words while spelling them, or even before beginning to spell them. At this point, advance to the Sweep-Sweep-Spell step.

2   SWEEP-SWEEP-SPELL

The purpose of Sweep-Sweep-Spell is to continue training in left-right eye movement and word recognition, Understanding what is read is *not* yet the goal. If you have been revealing the words rather than pointing them out, have the student slide the pieces of paper to reveal individual words and lines of text. As the student improves in the skills of word recognition and eye movement, get rid of the piece of paper that is slid left to right, and slide only one piece of paper down the page to reveal an entire line at a time.

The new instruction is: 'Let your eyes sweep through (or over) the word. If the word doesn't just come out of your mouth, sweep it again. If it doesn't come out of your mouth the second time, spell it. Then I'll tell you what it is, and you repeat it.'

At the first sign of any disorientation, cover the material with your hand and ask the student to check orientation.

Sincerely praise each sign of improvement.

If you are working with a child using a primer or first reader, use this step until most of the words are recognised while sweeping them. Then say, 'This book is too easy. We need to use something harder.' Increase the difficulty of the material one level at a time. At first the student may have some doubt or reservation about reading something harder. Say, 'If it's too hard, we can always come back.'

When the student can recognise almost every word at his or her appropriate scholastic level, switch to the next step: Picture-at-Punctuation.

3   PICTURE-AT-PUNCTUATION

The only purpose of reading is to understand what is read. Reading without full and complete comprehension of what is read is the source of most misunderstanding in any subject at any level.

The goal of Picture-at-Punctuation is full and complete comprehension of what is read.

In Western written languages, each complete thought is either followed by, or surrounded [bracketed] by punctuation marks. Each complete thought can be either pictured or felt.

Tell the student, 'We are now going to add meaning to what you're reading. To us, punctuation means "picture". When you see a punctuation mark, make a picture in your mind of what you have just read.'

Picture-at-Punctuation is an added step to Sweep-Sweep-Spell.

Point out the punctuation marks where the student should stop and form a mental picture:

- periods
- exclamation marks
- question marks
- commas
- quotation marks
- semicolons
- dashes
- parentheses or brackets
- colons

Have the student read a short sentence or clause (only the words leading up to the first punctuation mark). Stop the student from looking at the words just read. Cover the words with your hand if you need to.

Ask the student, 'What do you see?'

If the clause is something that cannot be pictured, like 'long ago', or 'once upon a time', ask, 'What do you feel?' or 'What does that mean to you?'

Sometimes you will encounter non-trigger words or unknown words for which the dyslexic student simply has no meaning. When this happens, you can explain the meaning of the word or look it up in a simple dictionary.

Some trigger words will cause disorientations. Point out that the word is a trigger word, say 'check your point' and pick up where the student left off. If she has already done Symbol Mastery on that word, you have hit a particular definition of the word that will also need to be mastered.

At some point, the student will start reading voluntarily for pleasure. Once you notice that someone is reading articles simply because they're interesting, your job is done. Do more coaching only if it is requested, and encourage the student to use Symbol Mastery for any words or expressions that cause confusion.

CHAPTER 33

Symbol Mastery for Words

Most people, including those without dyslexia, don't know the definitions of the common trigger words; even though they happen to be the most frequently used words in the English language. I have met English teachers who couldn't define *a* or *the* as other than 'articles'. Anyone's reading skill and comprehension will be vastly improved by mastering the definitions of these words.

NO CONCENTRATION ALLOWED

Symbol Mastery should be a playful, game-like activity. Consider that the words and symbols are little puzzles, with each definition forming a piece of the puzzle. Most dyslexics have had frustrating experiences at school, so many rely on rote memorisation to give the appearance of learning something. Building the forms of the letters in clay not only helps break the habit of heavy concentration, it allows the person to do something creative as a learning activity.

Whether you are doing Symbol Mastery by yourself or helping someone else with it, make it a learning experience. Make it all right to make mistakes and get things wrong sometimes. Finding mistakes is one of the best ways to learn things. Very few people have already studied or know all the definitions of these words.

If the student gets stumped on a certain word or symbol, just mark it for future reference and go on to one that is easy. If the going gets tedious, take a break and check for orientation.

Following are the Symbol Mastery steps and procedures for words, some hints on getting started, and the list of trigger words.

SYMBOL MASTERY PROCEDURE

1 Look up the word in a dictionary or glossary.

2 If you don't know how to pronounce it, find out.

3 Read the first definition and sample sentences aloud.

4 Establish a clear understanding of the definition. Discuss it. Make up sentences or phrases using the word with that definition.

the

1 that which is here or which has
   been mentioned.
   [*Give me the ball. Open the book.*]

2 that one of a number or group.
[*The man on the left is taller.
Take the one on top.*]

3 any one of a certain kind.
[*The orange is a fruit. The
elephant is a mammal.*]

Examples of how three definitions of the word **the** *can be
represented with Symbol Mastery*

5   Make a clay model of the concept described by the definition. How to make a clay model is described in the hints below.

6   Make the symbol or the letters of the word out of clay. Make sure the word is spelt correctly. Use lower case letters unless the word is a proper noun that is normally capitalised.

7   Make a mental picture of what has been created.

8   Say aloud to the model: 'This is (word), meaning (definition).'

(Example: 'This is *tall*, meaning *of more than normal height*.')

9   Say aloud to the word or symbol: 'This says (word).'

(Example: 'This says *tall*.')

Make up more sentences and phrases until you can do so easily. Be sure the usage of the word matches the definition you have just made.

These additional exercises are optional:

a   Touch and say the letters of the word.
b   Write the word.

Before diving into the small words, practise the

steps of Symbol Mastery on an easy word such as *lamb*, *apple*, or *cat*. Nouns tend to be easy to picture and make in clay. After that, try a verb or adjective such as *jump* or *tall*. This will get the student used to doing each of the steps.

Depending on the individual, there may be additional trigger words besides those listed below that need to be mastered. These could be key words in a difficult subject, words that are consistently misspelt, homonyms, new vocabulary, or words that are repeatedly misread. Just note them as they are encountered and add them to the list of words that need to be mastered.

SYMBOL MASTERY HINTS
FOR SMALL WORDS

The 'trigger' words listed below are those that most often cause confusion and disorientation when reading, writing, or communicating. They are confusing because:

a The person does not have a mental image of what the word means or represents.

b Many of these words have multiple meanings.

Here are ways to make mastering them easier:

1   Use a dictionary that gives sample sentences or phrases along with each definition.

2   Keep making up sample sentences and phrases with a particular definition until you are sure you know it and are comfortable using the word with that definition.

3   Start with words that have only a few definitions, such as the articles *a*, *an* and *the*; and the pronouns *I*, *you*, *me*, *we*, *him*, *her*, *this* and *that*.

4   Substitute the definition for the word itself in a phrase or sentence. This helps clarify the meaning so that you'll know if you are using the word correctly.

Example

The word *a* can mean 'one' or 'for each'. If you are doing the first definition where it means 'one' and your sentence is 'Eggs are £1.54 *a* dozen', you can substitute the definition 'one' for the word *a* in your sentence. 'Eggs are £1.54 *one* dozen' doesn't sound right or make sense. Using the other definition, 'for each', the substitution would be 'Eggs are £1.54 *for each* dozen', which is correct.

---

5   Master the first or major definition of each word on the list first, and create only two to four definitions per session. Doing too many

definitions at once will cause confusion. Once you have completed the first or major definition of each word, go through the list again and complete the rest of the definitions for each word.

6   If you hit a definition you can't make sense of, there is probably a word *within the definition itself* you don't understand. You can look up these words and master them, or look in another dictionary to see if it explains that particular definition more clearly.

7   The word *be*, and its other forms such as *is*, *was* and *are*, are the most difficult words on the list to master. Save them for last, and have a grammar book handy.

8   Make sure the clay figures and models you make are 'realistic'. This does not mean they have to be extremely artistic or exactly lifelike. It means they should be three-dimensional, and should represent physical reality in a recognisable way. They should not be overly abstract or symbolic. A blob of clay cannot be representative of a car; the blob must at least have four wheels.

9   A clay model of a person can be made to look like a stick figure, but it should be large and sturdy enough to stand on its own. When you need to show action or emotion, it needs

A child's definition of the word 'and'.

arms and legs that can be positioned, and a head that can have facial expressions carved into it.

10 Use clay arrows to show directions or sequence.

11 Make a clay rope into a 'cartoon bubble' that is attached to a person's head to show that something is an idea or is happening in the mind. Show what is going on in the mind within the borders of the 'bubble'.

12 Make the clay letters of the words in lower case 'printed' form, the way they most often appear in books. Only *I* and other proper names are always capitalised. Check to see that you have spelt the word correctly after you have made it out of clay.

A clay model of the word 'noun'.

13 Some words are grouped with their different tenses and forms. You should use a grammar book to understand them fully. This is an opportunity to learn and master what happens to a word when you add different endings to it such as *-ed*, *-s* and *-ing*, and also how words can change depending on whether you are talking about the present, the past or the future.

14 As you progress through the words, you may notice that the definitions of each word are grouped according to what kind of word they are (parts of speech: noun, adjective, adverb, verb, pronoun, conjunction, preposition or interjection). Looking in a grammar book and learning what these are can help make the differences between the definitions clearer.

15 If a definition seems hard or confusing, take a brief break. Look out of a window, stand up for a minute or just stretch your arms, and be sure to check orientation before continuing.

THE SMALL WORDS
The Key Triggers for Disorientation

NOTE: *Words with more than one form are in* **bold** *type, followed by their other forms.*

a	*back*	*by*	*each*
about	**be**	**can**	*either*
again	*am*	*could*	*else*
ago	*are*	*can't*	*even*
all	*is*	*cannot*	*ever*
almost	*was*	**come**	*every*
also	*were*	*came*	*everything*
always	*being*	*comes*	*for*
an	*been*	*coming*	*from*
and	*because*	**do**	*front*
another	**become**	*did*	*full*
any	*became*	*does*	**get**
anyhow	*becoming*	*doing*	*gets*
anyway	*becomes*	*done*	*getting*
as	*before*	*don't*	*got*
at	*between*	*doesn't*	**go**
away	*but*	*down*	*goes*

going	*its*	*making*	*onto*
gone	*it's*	*many*	*or*
went	*just*	*may*	*other*
have	*last*	*maybe*	*others*
had	***leave***	*me*	*otherwise*
has	*leaves*	*mine*	*our*
having	*leaving*	*more*	*ours*
he	*left*	*most*	*out*
he's	*least*	*much*	*over*
her	*less*	*my*	***put***
hers	***let***	*neither*	*puts*
here	*lets*	*never*	*putting*
him	*let's*	*no*	***run***
his	*letting*	*none*	*ran*
how	***like***	*nor*	*running*
I	*liked*	*not*	*runs*
if	*likes*	*now*	*same*
in	*liking*	*of*	***see***
into	***make***	*off*	*saw*
isn't	*made*	*on*	*seen*
it	*makes*	*one*	*sees*

she	took	through	which
she's	than	to	while
shall	that	too	who
should	that's	unless	who's
so	the	until	whose
some	their	up	why
soon	theirs	upon	will
stand	them	us	with
standing	then	very	within
stands	there	we	without
stood	there's	we're	won't
such	these	what	would
sure	they	when	yet
take	they're	where	you
takes	this	where's	your
taking	those	whether	you're
			yours

CHAPTER 34

Continuing the Process

The purpose of taking someone through the procedures described in the previous chapters is to correct the learning disability aspect of dyslexia.

The programme offered at our counselling centre takes an average of 30 hours. Most of that time is devoted to Symbol Mastery of the person's own unique triggering symbols. Our job is to train people in the skills for controlling their orientation, and help them to master the Symbol Mastery technique. Completing the words on the Small Words list is their assignment after completing our programme.

We also train a parent, spouse or other family member in basic tutoring techniques so that they can continue to offer support at home. People who go through the programme come back for one or more short 'tune-up' sessions.

The task of correction isn't really complete until the person's compulsive solutions no longer operate. So long as the person continues to use the old solutions, he or she might as well keep the old problem, because nothing will change permanently. So in order for dyslexia to be corrected, the old, compulsive solutions simply have to go.

The entire sequence of events that resulted in the person acquiring an old solution in the first place began because the person couldn't think with a trigger word. Mastering just the first or primary definition of a trigger word will allow the person to begin to think with that word non-verbally. That word will cease to cause an old solution to occur. As each word is mastered— even partially—the old solutions will fade away on their own.

The old solutions are no longer stimulated, so they don't automatically happen. As the person experiences life, he or she will discover things that work better than the old solutions did. As soon as the person experiences a better way of doing things, the old solutions are replaced.

The idea that deeply embedded compulsive behaviours can simply fall away on their own may sound incredible, but they do, especially in a patient, supportive environment. After a few months, most of them should disappear.

Experiencing the loss of an old solution is all the proof people need in order to know with certainty that their dyslexia is being corrected, and that the change is permanent.

This isn't to say dyslexics should master only the first or primary definitions of trigger words. That is when the old solutions begin to disappear, but a word isn't truly mastered until all its definitions are mastered. Dyslexics should exercise their *gift of mastery* and really get the job done thoroughly.

The person should also remember to check orientation whenever disorientation occurs for any reason. There will be things other than words in the person's life or environment that stimulate disorientation. These spontaneous disorientations aren't dyslexia, but they do share the same characteristics. They can often cause phobias. Orientation turns them *off*. However, fully dealing with phobias is not the subject of this book.

The person should also continue to master confusing words as they are encountered, using the Symbol Mastery procedure. This is a great way to study new subjects. In fact, for many corrected dyslexics attending colleges and universities, simply mastering the words in the glossaries of textbooks with this process has enabled them to achieve consistently high marks.

The final thought I want to leave you with is something I said at the end of Chapter 21.

*W*hen someone
masters something,
it becomes a part
of that person.
It becomes part of
the individual's thought
and creative process.
It adds the quality of
its essence to all
subsequent thought
and creativity of
the individual.

Ronald D. Davis
The Gift of Dyslexia
(415) 692-8990

Glossary

Acalculia: An inability to develop mathematical skills. *A person with acalculia cannot do arithmetic.*

ADD: acronym and abbreviation for attention deficit disorder.

ADHD: acronym and abbreviation for attention deficit hyperactivity disorder.

Agraphia: an inability to manipulate a writing instrument or express thoughts in writing. *A person with agraphia may speak well but cannot write.*

Alphabet: the letters of a language in their customary order. *The English alphabet has 26 letters.*

Attention: awareness of the environment. *Attention is what is used when enjoying a beautiful sunset.*

Attention Deficit Disorder: *see ADD.*

Balance: ability to stand on one foot without wobbling; a perception that can be used to check orientation. *By checking our balance we can tell if we are orientated.*

Concentration: limiting one's awareness to only one thing. *Heavy concentration produces a hypnotic state.*

Concept: an idea or thought; a mental picture; an idea of what something is, or what a group of things are. *Words are used to communicate a concept.*

Conceptualisation: an image, idea, thought or concept that is created in the mind; the act of mentally creating something. *Conceptualisation occurs in the mind.*

Confusion: an overwhelming feeling of blankness. *Confusion causes disorientation in dyslexics.*

Counselling: helping someone improve their abilities or get rid of their disabilities. *We get counselling when we need help with a problem.*

Davis Orientation Counselling: procedures which help a person create, find and use a stable location for the mind's eye; methods for controlling, monitoring and turning off disorientations. *Davis Orientation Counselling shows a person how to self-correct disorientations.*

Davis Orientation Counselling Programme: an individualised counselling programme where a person learns how to correct disorientations, maintain orientation and improve reading, writing, maths or attention focus skills. *The Davis Orientation Counselling Programme takes about 30 hours to complete.*

Davis Orientation Mastery: the overall name for the diagnostic, therapeutic and educational procedures developed by Ron Davis. *I trained in the Davis Orientation Mastery procedures.*

Davis Symbol Mastery: a procedure for learning what a symbol means, what it looks like and what it sounds like. *We create concepts with clay when we do Davis Symbol Mastery.*

Definition: a statement that tells the meaning of a word. *Tell me the definition of that word.*

Disorientate: to lose one's position or direction in relation to the true facts and conditions in the environment; to lose touch with reality to some degree. *People who disorientate easily sometimes feel dizzy.*

Disorientation: the loss of one's position or direction in relation to other things; a state of mind in which mental perceptions do not agree with the true facts and conditions in the environment; in some people, this is an automatic response to confusion. *During a disorientation the perceptions are altered.*

Dyscalculia: a form of dyslexia where the difficulty is primarily with maths and numbers. *A common symptom of dyscalculia is difficulty in learning phone numbers.*

Dysgraphia: a form of dyslexia where the difficulty is primarily with handwriting. *People with dysgraphia have problems with penmanship.*

Dyslexia: a type of disorientation caused by a natural cognitive ability which can replace normal sensory perceptions with conceptualisations; reading, writing, speaking or directional difficulties which stem from disorientations triggered by confusions regarding symbols. *Dyslexia stems from a perceptual talent.*

Dyspraxia: motor difficulties that can affect body movements. *Dyspraxia may present as clumsiness, handwriting problems or speech difficulties.*

Fine Tuning: the Davis procedure for checking and adjusting orientation using balance (described in Chapter 29). *Fine Tuning is done three days after an initial Orientation Counselling session.*

Holding: the phenomenon of trying to 'hold' the mind's eye in place. *Holding causes headaches.*

Hyperactivity: a condition that can accompany attention deficit disorder where a person appears overly restless, moves about a great deal and can't sit still. *Hyperactivity is the opposite of lethargy.*

Language: speech sounds that have meaning; written symbols that represent speech sounds; the speech and writing of a particular country or group of people. *The only language I know is English.*

Letter: a written symbol that represents a speech sound. *'Z' is a letter.*

Master: to know with certainty; to practise or do something until it is completely known. *To master something requires practice.*

Mastery: certainty; knowing for sure what something means, looks like or sounds like; knowing how to do something well; knowing without doubt. *His mastery of cooking makes him an excellent chef.*

Meaning: an idea someone has attached to an object. *All words have a meaning.*

Mind's eye: that which views one's mental images. *The mind's eye is what looks at our imagination.*

Natural orientation: a general location for the mind's eye that naturally occurs with human development. *A common natural orientation for a gymnast is a few metres directly above the head on midline.*

Non-verbal conceptualisation: thinking with mental pictures of concepts or ideas; any form of thinking that does not use words. *Intuition is a form of non-verbal conceptualisation.*

'Old Solutions': *see Solutions.*

Optimum orientation: placement of the mind's eye which results in all the perceptions being in agreement with each other and accurate; specifically the senses of balance, motion, vision, hearing and time. *Optimum orientation results from Fine Tuning.*

Orientate: to put oneself in the proper position and state of mind so one's mental perceptions agree with the true facts and conditions in the environment; to position the mind's eye above and behind the head in a stable location. *When we orientate ourselves, we can read better.*

Orientation: putting oneself in the proper position in relation to the true facts and conditions; a state of mind in which mental perceptions agree with the true facts and conditions in the environment. *Orientation makes me feel less confused.*

Orientation Point: a stable location above and behind the head (this location varies from person to person). *Put your mind's eye on the orientation point.*

Perception: information that comes to the brain through the sensory organs and channels. *We determine what is real with our perception.*

Release: a relaxation and stress relief procedure (described in Chapter 28). *Do release when you feel tense.*

Review: a procedure used after Orientation Counselling to check if the orientation point is located in the proper place. *Do Review with the student at least once a day.*

Solutions (compulsive): behaviours, habits and mental tricks adopted to resolve the mistakes and frustrations caused by disorientation; the components of a learning disability. *Having to sing the Alphabet Song is a common solution to not being able to learn the alphabet.*

Stable orientation: a condition in which a person's mind's eye tends to remain in one location most or all of the time. *People who do not experience dyslexic symptoms tend to have a stable orientation.*

Symbol: something that means or represents something else. *The flag is a symbol of our country.*

Threshold for confusion: the point at which the confusion in the environment becomes overwhelming to an individual. *When dyslexics reach their threshold for confusion, they become disorientated.*

Trigger (word): anything that causes disorientation; usually a word or symbol for which a person does not have a complete or accurate concept. *The word 'the' is a common trigger word.*

Unstable orientation: a condition in which a person's mind's eye moves about a lot. *People who experience motion sickness easily tend to have an unstable orientation.*

Verbal conceptualisation: thinking with the sounds of words. *Hearing your thoughts in words is a form of verbal conceptualisation.*

Word: a spoken sound, or letters that represent that sound, which have a meaning or definition in a language. *I learned a new word today.*

Recommended References

The programme described in this book will be most successful if the student and support person work with reference books that feel right for them. The books listed below have been found to be compatible with, and suitable for, the Davis methods and are the best we have found so far that are readily available in the United Kingdom.

However, you may well find a new book—or have an old favourite—that is not on the list but which works particularly well for you. DDA-UK would always like to hear from anyone who has found something that has proved especially useful, so that we can add it to our list of suggestions.

DICTIONARIES

The following dictionaries are recommended in order of complexity; however, any one of them is suitable for any age.

The first two do not have pronunciation guides, but the definitions in them are clear and straightforward to work from for Symbol Mastery, particularly when one is getting started.

The Oxford Primary School Dictionary
The Oxford School Dictionary
The Oxford Wordpower Dictionary
The Concise Oxford Dictionary
The Oxford Advanced Learners Dictionary

All the above are published by Oxford University Press.

GRAMMAR

The books listed below contain all you need to know in the way of the basics of English grammar, in various formats, any one of them being suitable for any age.

Know all about Grammar and Punctuation (Key Stage Two), Ladybird.
Cartoons and colour with good descriptions, plus ideas and exercises to do to practise your new-found knowledge. A neat, mini-reference paperback is provided in the centre of the book to pull out and keep, which also has plenty of colour and cartoons.

English Grammar
Punctuation
Both compiled by the National Confederation of Parent-Teacher Associations Home Learning, and published by Hodder.
Clear, good descriptions, plus exercises, for those who wish to consolidate their knowledge. No-nonsense type layout printed in blue, and not a picture in sight!

Handling Language I
Handling Language II
Handling Punctuation
All three by John Davis, published by Stanley Thornes.
A comprehensive set of books, with easy-to-use contents/ index page, some colour and good cartoons.

Fowler's Modern English Usage, Oxford University Press.
The ultimate guide to grammar, syntax, punctuation and usage. A classic that should be in every home, it will not only

help to settle arguments about correct usage but is highly entertaining in its own right.

RECOMMENDED READING

ADHD: How to Deal with Very Difficult Children, Alan Train, Souvenir Press.
Practical, sympathetic advice for parents and teachers, explaining what ADHD is, how it affects children and what can be done to help them learn techniques of self-control that will enable them to cope with their condition.

THE GIFT OF DYSLEXIA
is also available on audio tape

For those who would prefer to listen rather than read, a cassette version is available. It is narrated by the author, Ron Davis, and consists of three 90-minute cassettes. *When listening you will need to refer to this book*, as the author alludes to numerous diagrams and illustrations.

To obtain the audio version, send £20.00 (including postage and packing) to: DDA-UK, PO Box 40, Winchester, Hampshire SO22 6ZH.
Tel: 01962 881987.
Fax: 01962 886997.
email: england@dyslexia.com

Also available: a set of three instructional videotapes demonstrating the Davis Assessment, Orientation and Symbol Mastery Procedures. Total running time, 3½ hours. Send £80.00 (including postage and packing) to the above address.

Overseas postage rates for the audio and videotapes available on application.

Davis Dyslexia Association
International (DDAI)

DDAI oversees activities for all DDA affiliates, and arranges events in the United States, Canada, Australia and all other areas not serviced by a local DDA. DDAI also oversees and maintains certification standards worldwide for Davis practitioners. For information about training or services utilising the Davis dyslexia correction methods, please contact the following organisations, or visit DDAI's website at http://www.dyslexia.com/

UNITED STATES

DDAI
1601 Old Bayshore Highway, Suite 245, Burlingame,
   CA 94010.
Tel: 00 1 (415) 692-8995
Toll-free in US and Canada: 1-888-999-3324
Fax: 00 1 (415) 692-7075
email: ddai@dyslexia.com

Reading Research Council – Dyslexia Correction Center
1601 Old Bayshore Highway, Suite 260, Burlingame,
   CA 94010.
Tel: 00 1 (415) 692-8990
Toll-free in US and Canada: 1-800-729-8990
Fax: 00 1 (415) 692-8997
email: RRCdcc@ao1.com

UNITED KINGDOM

DDA-UK
PO Box 40, Winchester, Hampshire SO22 6ZH.
Tel: (00 44) 01962 881987
Fax: (00 44) 01962 886997
email: england@dyslexia.com

HOLLAND

DDA-Nederland
Kerkweg 38a, 6105 CG Maria Hoop.
Tel: 00 31 (0)475 301 277
Fax: 00 31 (0)475 301 381
email: holland@dyslexia.com

GERMANY

DDA-Deutschland
Conventstrasse 14, 22089 Hamburg.
Tel: 00 49 (0)40 25 17 86 22
Fax: 00 49 (0)40 25 17 86 24
email: germany@dyslexia.com

SWITZERLAND

DDA-CH
Freie Strasse 81, 4001 Basel.
Tel: 00 41 (0)61 272 24 00
Fax: 00 41 (0)61 272 42 41
email: switzerland@dyslexia.com

MEXICO

DDA-Mexico
Rio Missouri 118 Ote, Colonia del Valle, Garza Garcia,
  Monterrey, Nuevo Leon 66220.
Tel/Fax: 00 52 (8) 378-0987 or 00 52 (8) 335-9435
email: mexico@dyslexia.com

Index

ADD, 54–60
ability assessment, 128
acalculia, 43
agraphia, 47
alphabet, 70
alphabet mastery, 202–8
Alphabet Song, 30, 67, 70, 202
anchor lines, 155–8, 173
Andersen, Hans Christian, 4
assessment procedure, 128,
    141–50
attention, 56–7
attention deficit disorder, 54–60
  with hyperactivity, 59–60
autism, 70, 74, 110, 112

balance, sense of, 60, 61–3, 79,
    126, 188–9, 194
Bell, Alexander Graham, 4
boredom, 43, 57–8

Cher, 4
child development, 73–95
Churchill, Winston, 4
clay modelling, 198–233
clumsiness, 61–3, 195
cognizance, 101
comfort zone, 188
concentration, 31, 54, 217
  vs. attention, 31, 56
confusion, 55, 79, 198
coordination problems, 126, 195
coordination process, 195–7
crawling treatment, 107
creativity, 68–70, 109–12
curiosity, 106–8

da Vinci, Leonardo, 4, 104–5
Davis Orientation Counselling,
    65
  implementation, 135–40
  procedure, 134, 151–79
  programme, 237
Davis Orientation Mastery, 141
Davis Perceptual Ability
    Assessment, 134, 141–50
Davis Symbol Mastery, 41,
    66–7, 114 (see also Symbol
    Mastery)
daydreaming, 58, 100
dictionaries, recommended,
    250–1
dictionary, 36
  use of, 225
Disney, Walt, 4, 5
disorientation, 15–20, 55–60,
    64–6, 121
  ability, 76
  defined, 14
  effects of, 102–4, 124–7
  triggers for, 198
dopamine, 44
dyscalculia, 43
dysgraphia, 47–50
dyslexia, 3, 6, 8
  as learning disability, 8–14
  as talent, 99–105
  hereditary, 73
  symptoms, 20, 66, 87, 119–23,
    125–8
dyslexic adults, 92–4
dyslexic children, 3, 73–92
dyspraxia, 61–3, 195

Edison, Thomas, 4
Einstein, Albert, 4, 5, 100, 102
eyes, 15, 102
   flicker-fusion rate, 101–3

Fine Tuning, 187–94

gift of mastery, 99, 113–15,
   239–41
Goldberg, Whoopi, 4
Goodhew, Duncan, 4
grammar book, 209, 230, 232,
   251

Hampshire, Susan, 4, 5
handwriting, 47–53, 126
headaches, 181, 183
hearing, 126
Heseltine, Michael, 4
holding, 181
hyperactivity, 59–60, 126
hypnotism, 27–8

incidence of awareness, 101, 103
infancy, 73–7
intuitive thought, 5, 32, 76, 98,
   101–3
invalidation, 87–9

Kosslyn, Stephen, 77

languages, differences in, 38–9
learning disability, 70
   anatomy of, 120–3

mastering words, 224–36
mastering words, example, 226,
   231, 232
mastery, 113–15, 239–41
maths problems, 43–6, 212

mind's eye, 16, 129–34, 141–50,
   154–79, 180–6, 189–92
motion, sense of, 60, 61–3
multidimensional thinking, 5,
   87, 104

neural pathways, 48–52
non-verbal conceptualisation,
   9–12, 82–3, 100–1

orientation, 15, 65
Orientation Counselling
   procedure (*see* Davis
   Orientation Counselling)
orientation point, 159–65
   defined, 159
   illustration, 159, 165, 173
   optimum, 133, 187–94
Orientation Review procedure,
   184–6, 194
Orton, Samuel, T., 8

Patton, General George, 4
perception, 104–5
   altering and creating, 5, 18, 77
phonetics (*see* Pronunciation
   Mastery)
phonics, 35
Piaget, Jean, 72
Picture-at-Punctuation, 221–3
Pronunciation Mastery, 210–1
Punctuation Mastery, 208–10

reading, 34–9, 215–23
release procedure, 182–4
responsibility, 175
Ritalin, 59

sculpting, 94
self-esteem, 3, 88, 91, 93
serifs, 212

Smith, Joan, ix
solutions, compulsive or 'old',
    29–33, 68–9, 90–3, 122,
    127, 238
sounds, 126
spelling, 40–2
Spell-Reading, 215–21
Stewart, Jackie, 4
subliminal thought, 101–3
Sweep-Sweep-Spell, 220–1
Symbol Mastery, 66–9, 198–214,
    224–36
Symbol Mastery hints, 228—33
symbols vs. objects, 85

time, sense of, 43–6
thought, multidimensional, 5,
    87, 104

thought, non-verbal, 9–14,
    100–1
thought, verbal, 9–13, 82, 100
threshold for confusion, 14
trigger word list, 22, 234–6
trigger words, 21–8, 66–7,
    214
typefaces, 37–8, 211–12
typography, 35–6

verbal conceptualisation, 9–12,
    82, 100–1

word mastery, 224–36
writing, 47–53

Yeats, W. B., 4